AF207297

Denkart Europa | Mindset Europe

Denkart Europa|Mindset Europe presents international academic analyses and contributions on a broad range of Europe-related subjects. The book series addresses the general public worldwide and contributes to the reflection on political and societal developments in Europe. With Denkart Europa|Mindset Europe, the foundation ASKO Europa-Stiftung and Europäische Akademie Otzenhausen present the outcomes of their versatile activities. Its monographies, anthologies, essays and handbooks invite to a continuous interdisciplinary discourse on Europe.

edited by ASKO Europa-Stiftung, Saarbrücken and Europäische Akademie Otzenhausen.

European Horizons [Ed.]

Cornerstones for an Evolving Europe

New Policy Approaches to Economic Development,
Environmental Policy, and Human Rights

 **Nomos**

The Deutsche Nationalbibliothek lists this publication in the
Deutsche Nationalbibliografie; detailed bibliographic data
are available on the Internet at http://dnb.d-nb.de

ISBN   978-3-8487-8552-0 (Print)
        978-3-7489-2913-0 (ePDF)

British Library Cataloguing-in-Publication Data
A catalogue record for this book is available from the British Library.

ISBN   978-3-8487-8552-0 (Print)
        978-3-7489-2913-0 (ePDF)

Library of Congress Cataloging-in-Publication Data
European Horizons
Cornerstones for an Evolving Europe
New Policy Approaches to Economic Development,
Environmental Policy, and Human Rights
European Horizons (Ed.)
129 pp.
Includes bibliographic references.

ISBN   978-3-8487-8552-0 (Print)
        978-3-7489-2913-0 (ePDF)

Onlineversion
Nomos eLibrary

1st Edition 2022
© Nomos Verlagsgesellschaft, Baden-Baden, Germany 2022. Overall responsibility
for manufacturing (printing and production) lies with Nomos Verlagsgesellschaft mbH
& Co. KG.

This work is subject to copyright. All rights reserved. No part of this publication may
be reproduced or transmitted in any form or by any means, electronic or mechanical,
including photocopying, recording, or any information storage or retrieval system,
without prior permission in writing from the publishers. Under § 54 of the German
Copyright Law where copies are made for other than private use a fee is payable to
"Verwertungsgesellschaft Wort", Munich.

No responsibility for loss caused to any individual or organization acting on or refraining
from action as a result of the material in this publication can be accepted by Nomos
or the editor.

Table of Contents

Foreword

Nidhi Menon, Laurent Bélanger-Lowe, and Pierre Nouailletas-Baneth

For the past two years, Covid-19 has dominated political discourse, economic policymaking, and the human experiences of communities across the globe. In so doing, the pandemic has not only reignited dialogues on issues that are of critical importance to the European Union, but also exposed serious vulnerabilities in its political and economic systems.

While recovery efforts are focused on addressing the short-term economic damage caused by Covid-19, the EU must consider how this can be a pivotal moment that enables long-term change. The EU must address the evolving challenges of the global economic situation, certainly. But it must also tackle its vulnerabilities with transformative policies that can bring about a more sustainable, equitable, and successful Union.

Indeed, this period of uncertain economic recovery can become a critical juncture in the EU's history. It provides a window of opportunity for the EU to take on a more assertive role abroad and a more intentional approach at home, and in so doing lay the cornerstones for a better future. This collection of essays explores how Europe might lay these cornerstones.

Inaugurated by Arroyo Nieto's critical piece, the collection begins by considering the EU's 'foundational myth'—the post-war reconciliation between France and Germany—and where it leaves us today.

The need for a pan-European cultural dialogue that Arroyo Nieto concludes on is taken up by Bernoville, who examines the potential of Von der Leyen's New European Bauhaus initiative. Indeed, she proposes that the New Bauhaus can create a tangible narrative connecting European citizens on critical topics, particularly the transformational approach of the European Green Deal.

The collection's third piece digs deeper into the European Green Deal's promise, this time examining a seldom discussed and yet high-impact aspect of the deal. The EU's forest policy—currently in a watershed moment, Bayne argues—has the potential, if delivered correctly, to deliver both a win for climate mitigation and increased cohesion and cooperation between Member States.

Yet no discussion of the European Green Deal could neglect the imperiled state of climate ambition in the face of today's geopolitical turmoil in Ukraine. Blair's piece assesses this present moment, taking Germany as a case study to propose forward-looking avenues for renewable energy investment in the EU.

Recognizing that the EU's climate ambition must transcend its own internal policies, Simintzis's piece builds on Blair's by examining how the EU can externalize its climate policies, and ensure that the so-called Brussels Effect actually does spur the adoption of EU standards abroad.

In pursuing this more muscular role overseas, the EU must carefully consider how it can leverage its allies to advance value-based outcomes. Evergreen's piece tackles this question by examining the implications of EU and US relations with China. A strong transatlantic bond, she concludes, is an indispensable aspect of a more global Europe.

At the same time, Europe's global role cannot be exclusively outward-looking. Indeed, the chaos caused by the Covid-19 pandemic has damaged the EU's brand. In her piece, Ghosh examines how the global community—and the EU in particular—has violated a central tenet of the global framework for refugees.

Thakker's piece supplements this view with a broader analysis of how the EU's migration policies have evolved during the course of the pandemic, concluding that the EU needs a more coherent approach.

This need for coherence, once again made clear during the EU's uneven Covid-19 response, is explored in greater detail by Asghar's piece. Exposing a severe lack of preparedness across countries and institutions, Ashgar proposes a way forward, a new framework for European crisis and disaster management.

A key aspect of this new framework is greater citizen inclusion, which is at once critical in creating rapid and effective response measures, and in ensuring their political and ethical legitimacy. The imperative to create a more genuinely inclusive way of engaging citizens—a motif throughout this collection—is tackled by its last piece, in which Wong outlines how Europe can design its cities for meaningful public participation that goes beyond the largely symbolic roles that currently exist for citizens. To do so, Europe must look beyond conventional ideas of empowerment and design its cities for trust; only then will the EU be able to bridge the gap between citizens and policymakers.

This is the very gap that we tirelessly work to narrow at European Horizons. We firmly believe in Europe's potential as a force for good, and want to harness the bold and innovative spirit of today's young transatlantic leaders—the catalyst we think is needed to drive meaningful change in an often intractable world. We hope this book will play its small part in helping European leaders conceptualize, design, and implement policy solutions that champion the aspirations and values of the European Union.

On behalf of European Horizons,
Nidhi Menon, *Director of Publications*
Pierre Nouailletas-Baneth, *Deputy Director of Publications*
Laurent Bélanger-Lowe, *Executive Director*

Conference on the Past of Europe: The EU's foundational myth and where it leaves us today

José María Arroyo Nieto

Introduction

In his famous book about the development of nationalism, *Imagined Communities*, Benedict Anderson defined the nation as "an imagined political community – and imagined as both inherently limited and sovereign…It is imagined because the members of even the smallest nation will never know most of their fellow-members, meet them, or even hear of them, yet in the minds of each lives the image of their communion".[1] Every community is built around a series of identifying symbols that show who its members are, what it represents, and what it stands for. Nations take pride in their national symbols, monuments, institutions, and achievements. Frequently, these unifying elements are key components of a historical narrative that binds the community's present with its past and projects it into the future. Together these factors comprise a community's identity, essentially providing the entire population with a shared reply to the question "who are we?". This identity is often summarized in a foundational myth, a short story that, while rooted in some historical facts, mainly serves the purpose of reinforcing the community. These myths do not always go uncontested nor are they always totally in line with historical events, but they are important to society. In this paper, I will explain and analyse the European Union's foundational myth, explore the controversies it has created, and determine whether it is possible or advisable to adapt it to 21st century Europe.

The EU's Foundational Myth

As a human institution, the European Union is subject to the desire for meaningful origins, which is similarly sought out in organisations and

---

1 Anderson Benedict R, *Imagined Communities: Reflections on the Origin and Spread of Nationalism* (London: Verso, 2016), 6.

nations around the world. While often seen as a purely bureaucratic or technocratic organisation, the EU has always had clear political and social aims, some of them extremely disruptive. These include fostering peace, democracy, prosperity, unity, and integration among the European peoples. Leading up to the foundational 1957 Treaty of Rome, European policymakers intended to "lay the foundations of an ever-closer union among the peoples of Europe".[2] This ambitious and somewhat controversial goal required a very strong narrative for people to accept it.

The myth that justifies the existence of the EU is best summarised at the European Parliament's exhibition centre Parlamentarium in Brussels, as quoted by Finnish professor Tuuli Lähdesmäki in her article on the *Founding Myths of EU Europe*:

> "For decades, the stage of Europe progressed under the same principle: Each nation for itself. Countries fought to secure their own interests with force, if necessary. The dreadful consequences of this approach were the two World Wars. By the end of the Second World War the continent is in ruins with widespread mistrust and increasing desperation. Yet for one group of prominent and forward-looking politicians the solution is clear: the ideas of the past must be discarded. Despite the new major threat looming—the Cold War between the USA and the Soviet Union—they dare to make a fresh start. In their vision, those in charge will stop pointing weapons at one another and instead take their seats around the same table in the name of consensus and cooperation, thus paving the way for a peaceful and prosperous Europe. This vision brought about the first decisive steps toward the Schumann declaration. At this table you will discover just how this document of utmost importance for Europe's future came to be and how the world reacted.[3]

As this paragraph suggests, the EU claims to trace its origins to the Second World War, and more specifically, to the aftermath of the conflict in Europe. In this narrative, 1945 was "year zero" for the new Europe. After two devastating wars in only three decades, most of the continent lay in ruins. Millions of people had been killed and the risk of further conflict

---

2 Hunnings, Neville March, and Joe Macdonald Hill. *The Treaty of Rome Consolidated and the Treaty of Maastricht*. London: European Law Centre at Sweet & Maxwell, 1992.
3 Lähdesmäki, Tuuli. "Founding Myths of EU Europe and the Workings of Power in the EU Heritage and History Initiatives." European Journal of Cultural Studies 22, no. 5–6 (October 2019): 789.

could not be dismissed. After all, the previous World War, as well as the peace treaties that followed it, had not kept Europeans from fighting each other again only a few years after.

The immediate post-war years were a turning point. It was clear that "peacekeeping" systems of the past had been unsuccessful, so there was a window of opportunity to try something new. In order to address the threat of a Third World War, leaders in Western Europe decided to try a new alternative: instead of signing treaties on paper that could easily be broken, they would build a new community with permanent structures. This would make Europeans depend on each other for economic prosperity and diminish the risk of a new conflict. The new Community was largely based on Franco-German reconciliation. In 1951, only six years after the surrender of the German Army, France, West Germany, Italy, Belgium, the Netherlands, and Luxembourg cooperated in the creation of the European Coal and Steel Community. From then on, integration only deepened, and the European Community would continue to grow into the organization of 27 Member States it is today.

Challenges

This narrative, however long standing and successful, faces several challenges. It is essentially true that the "Founding Fathers" of the EU, Jean Monnet, Robert Schuman, Konrad Adenauer, Alcide de Gasperi and others, wanted to build a new and peaceful Europe that would break the cycle of perpetual conflict. It is also true that they took bold and very innovative steps to move towards said goals. After decades of intermittent wars in Europe, they decided to move forward with a new community that would intertwine the destinies of its member states forever, significantly reducing the likelihood of renewed conflict. Notwithstanding all this, this narrative from the late 1940s and 1950s conveniently ignores several factors that contributed decisively to European peace and integration in the same time period.

To begin with the most obvious one, it completely neglects the role the US played in this foundational moment. A recent column in *The Economist* by Duncan Robinson explored the key role of American presence in post-war Europe in making the continent what it is today. He even claims that Harry Truman, under whose administration the Marshall Plan (officially named the European Recovery Program) was enacted, should be included as one of the "Founding Fathers of Europe".[4] The Marshall Plan was certainly one of the driving factors that led to the creation of the ECSC, as Washington wanted Europeans to be united and coordinated in their recovery efforts to better oppose the Soviet Union.

In addition to this political and financial commitment, and in contrast to decisions made between 1918–1920, the US chose to keep its military presence in Western Europe following agreement with host countries. After the defeat of Nazi Germany, the main threat to peace in Europe was not a resurgent and vindicative Germany, as many people feared at the time, but a new war with the Soviet Union in the context of the Cold War. This threat was very close to becoming a reality several times in Europe, most notably during the 1948–1949 Berlin Blockade. While the nascent European Community played a positive role in reducing tensions between its members, it could have done little to stand up to the USSR if conflict sprang anew. Individual European countries were simply not strong enough to face the Soviets on their own. It was only the continued military alliance with the US through NATO that kept Stalin and his successors at bay.

Therefore, the history of the EU is inextricably linked to that of the US and the Atlantic Alliance. Without it, the context in which Monnet, Schuman, Adenauer and others built the Common Market, may simply not have existed. Observably, the US did not support Western Europe with money and troops out of generosity towards Europeans or idealism. Among other reasons, they strategically wanted to keep Moscow in check, and sought to promote transatlantic trade. But the EU's foundational myth glosses over the key contribution of the American allies towards post-war peace in Western Europe. It naively claims that peace in Europe was kept because "those in charge stop[ped] pointing weapons at one another and instead [took] their seats around the same table in the name of consensus and cooperation, thus paving the way for a peaceful and prosperous Europe". Those in charge very much kept pointing weapons at each other in post-1945 Europe. However, it was mainly Americans and Soviets doing so at, but on European soil.

To this day, the EU-NATO relationship is a source of debate and controversy on both sides of the Atlantic. However, it is clear that today's modern Europe could not have existed without the US's support. Ignoring this

---

4 "The EU: Made in America," The Economist (The Economist Newspaper), accessed April 23, 2022, https://www.economist.com/europe/2021/06/17/the-eu-made -in-america

does little service to truth and may lead to erroneous conclusions about the present as well as the right way forward for Europe.

A second area in which the foundational myth is contested relates to the relationship between European nations and their colonies after 1945. In another sign of naiveté, the foundational myth is grounded on the idea that wars would be, following the Second World War, a thing of the past. Conflicts between nations would still exist but they would be resolved through dialogue and negotiation. Again, this approach was a remarkable success for relations between the six founding Members. Unfortunately, the will to solve conflicts through peaceful means did not extend to Europe's overseas colonies.

The post-war period is often seen as one of decolonization, where Europe realized it could no longer keep a hold on its empire and decided to grant independence to the colonies. However, decolonisation was certainly not a given after the war. Countries including France and The Netherlands fought long and bloody wars to keep their colonies while they were building a peaceful continent in Europe. Most notably, France did not see a contradiction between colonialism and European integration, particularly in the case of Algeria, which was part of the European Economic Community by way of French membership. French governments at the time had a very different view of what France, and therefore Europe, ought to be. As Timothy Snider put it, the countries that founded the EU (with the notable exception of Luxembourg) were all "dying empires" and that is a dimension of post-war history that should not be overlooked.[5] Again, the EU's foundational story ignores this part of history, since it does not fit well into the overall narrative of a peaceful and prosperous continent newly respectful of fundamental values and human rights.

A third criticism towards this myth is that it mainly focuses on the history of Western Europe. 1945 is certainly a key year for Germans, French, Belgians, Italians, and others. For the victors, it meant the end of German occupation and the recovery of their national independence. For the Germans, it meant the end of Nazism, a return to democracy, and their reincorporation into the West.

Nonetheless, for Central and Eastern Europeans, 1945 only meant the replacement of Nazi or Nazi allied governments with Soviet rule. It represented the beginning of four decades of foreign interference and totalitari-

---

5 Timothy Snyder, "Europe's Dangerous Creation Myth," POLITICO (POLITICO, May 1, 2019), https://www.politico.eu/article/europe-creation-project-myth-history -nation-state/

anism. The results of the Second World War also led to these states being cut off from the rest of Europe via the iron curtain. It was only between 1989–1991 that these states began to truly regain their independence and freedom. Myths are useful when they can unite society towards a common goal. But in this case, the origin story leaves out an important number of current Member States. For the first few decades of the EU the story made sense to the founding members, but nowadays it may contribute to existing disagreements between East and West.

It is true that EU institutions have tried to include the fall of the Berlin Wall as a new "foundational moment" for Europe. But since myths are also useful for education, this still begs the question: should a Polish high school student today care about what Monnet, Schuman and others did in the 1940s and 1950s? After all, Poland was occupied by the Soviets and would not take part in the European project until 2004. It is difficult to agree on a common narrative that is inclusive enough because of the diverse, often conflicting historical experiences and collective memories of the different European peoples.[6]

A fourth and possibly more pressing challenge to the aforementioned foundational EU narrative is the fact that it is becoming old and even outdated. In 1957, when the Treaty of Rome was signed, almost every European had lived through one or even two world wars. The idea that Europeans should come together to avoid further conflict clearly resonated with many people at the time. Nowadays, few people remain who can remember the war. Arguments noting that a united Europe helps avoid the possibility of war resonate less for the simple reason that younger people cannot even imagine a war-torn continent. As Joseph HH Weiler and Johann Justus Vasel explain in *The History of the European Union: Constructing Utopia*, "Europe became a victim of its own success: its achievement in making war unthinkable as a means for resolving differences has been so compelling that to new generations acculturated with this culture of peace, the sense of achievement has disappeared: it is taken for granted".[7] In this sense, the foundational tale may be self-defeating. Since war in Europe (or at least war between EU countries) is unthinkable nowadays, the EU may come to be seen as void of purpose.

---

6 Peter J. Verovsek, *Memory and the Future of Europe: Rupture and Integration in the Wake of Total War* (S.l.: MANCHESTER UNIV PRESS, 2022).

7 Giuliano Amato, *The History of the European Union. Constructing Utopia* (Oxford: Hart Publishing, 2019), p. 547.

A fifth criticism one could make is that the EU's origin story is based exclusively on Europe's most recent history (post 1945). The EU's "memory" or narrative of pre-1945 Europe is a universally negative one: one of "each nation for itself". In this sense, the Union sets itself against the past. It sees the past as a problem to be solved: nothing in it is worth remembering except as a lesson for how not to do things. Only European integration is worth any consideration. This makes the EU very vulnerable to attacks on its legitimacy. Nations, religious organisations, and other human institutions try to look for legitimacy in History, as far back as possible. They look for figures that could be seen as their forerunners. In particular, supporters of a stronger nation-state can always use the underlying idea that the nation is an institution legitimised by history while the EU is just an experiment with no strong roots or foundations.

EU leaders and the EU's identity

While these debates may appear academic and with few consequences for the day-to-day affairs of Member States or the European Union, they are becoming increasingly prominent in public discourse, to the point where they can make or break electoral campaigns. This was undoubtedly the case in the 2016 Brexit referendum. While there were strong economic arguments against leaving the EU and its Single Market, Leave backers succeeded in focusing the debate on British identity and history and arguing that the UK did not need the EU to succeed.[8] Supporters of remaining in the EU had few resources to counter this. They could not successfully counter the idea of "taking back control", that is, of returning to a past in which the nation had control over all its affairs.[9] During the French presidential campaign, much of the public debate has similarly been centered on France's, and to some extent Europe's, identity.[10] In both cases identity seems to be inevitably linked to the nation's future.

---

8 Chan, TW, Henderson, M, Sironi, M, Kawalerowicz, J. Understanding the social and cultural bases of Brexit. Br J Sociol. 2020; 71: 830- 851. https://doi.org/10.1111/1468-4446.12790

9 Joe Humphreys, "'Take Back Control': Why the Brexit Slogan Resonates across Europe," The Irish Times (The Irish Times, March 19, 2019), https://www.irishtimes.com/culture/take-back-control-why-the-brexit-slogan-resonates-across-europe-1.3824393

10 France 24, "French Election Year Kicks off with EU Flag Fracas at Paris's Arc De Triomphe," France 24 (France 24, January 3, 2022), https://www.france24.com/en

Furthermore, while these identity issues are constantly and passionately debated at the national level, they are extremely challenging for EU institutions to discuss. With a Union of 27 States, it is difficult to make any declaration without running the risk of potentially displeasing a member. Often, when EU leaders have ventured into these unexplored cultural territories beyond the official foundational myth described above, the result is controversial at best. Such was the case in 2018 when former President of the Commission Jean-Claude Juncker decided to pay homage to German philosopher Karl Marx on his 200th birthday in Trier. This may not have been particularly controversial in Juncker's home country Luxembourg. However in countries belonging to the former Soviet sphere of influence such as Poland, it did not go down particularly well.[11]

In another example showing glaring lack of sensitivity, former European Parliament President Antonio Tajani, while commemorating the World War II Foibe massacre, made certain remarks where he appeared to be designate Slovenian and Croatian territories as Italian. This drew sharp criticism from said countries, whose governments felt insulted and threatened by such statements, especially coming from a person representing the EU as a whole.[12]

Only last year, Maltese Commissioner for Equality Helena Dalli stirred an uncharacteristically passionate debate in the European Parliament, when a document containing "internal guidelines on inclusive language" was leaked to the press. The guidelines suggested avoiding use of the word "Christmas" when referring to the holidays that take place around the 25 December. MEPs, particularly from the centre-right such as François-Xavier Bellamy, accused her of wilfully neglecting Europe's Christian roots and culture.[13] In some way, this was a long overdue continuation of the 2000 s debate on whether the proposed (and then failed) European consti-

---

/france/20220103-french-election-year-kicks-off-with-eu-flag-fracas-at-paris-landmark

11 "En Pologne, L'hommage à Karl Marx Suscite L'incompréhension," Courrier international, May 7, 2018, https://www.courrierinternational.com/article/en-polo gne-lhommage-karl-marx-suscite-lincomprehension

12 Jacopo Barigazzi, "Slovenian, Croatian Leaders Accuse Tajani of 'Historical Revisionism'," POLITICO (POLITICO, April 18, 2019), https://www.politico.eu/articl e/slovenian-croatian-leaders-accuse-tajani-of-historical-revisionism/

13 Maïa de La Baume, "Eu Accused of Trying to Cancel Christmas! Advice on Inclusive Language Dropped after Criticism," POLITICO (POLITICO, December 1, 2021), https://www.politico.eu/article/european-commission-cancel-christmas-i nclusive-language-lgbtq/

tution should have had a reference to Europe's Christian roots (which it did not in the end).[14]

In summary, interaction with issues such as identity, collective memory, history, and culture have not yielded very positive results for EU leaders. When they have dared to address these issues, they have stirred unnecessary controversies by revealing their own national or partisan ideals, which subsequently, are ill-received by a sizeable number of EU citizens. This is one of the reasons why Commissioners and EU policymakers tend to keep an essentially technocratic profile. They are required to think "European", and doing so is interpreted as being a technocrat. When they need to address these cultural topics, they stick to the official foundational myth, no matter the possible controversies surrounding it. As a result, the foundational story remains immutable despite the many changes Europe has gone through in recent decades.

Admittedly, it is difficult to debate these issues in a highly fragmented and diverse Europe. But they are at the root cause of many topics that dominate headlines in 2022. Matters such as "European values", the rule of law, the primacy of EU law, the role of the Commission and the Parliament in national politics. Without getting to the core of the issues, these discussions become a repetition of mantras that are rarely fruitful.

Conclusion

Recently, the EU launched its Conference on the Future of Europe. The aim of this "pan-European democratic exercise" is to collect ideas from citizens on what they want Europe to look like in a few years.[15] This, pro-European optimists claim, could lead to a new round of integration. Most analysts, however, have underlined the lack of enthusiasm in national capitals and even in Brussels for treaty revisions or any type of profound restructuring of the EU.[16]

---

14 "L'Europe Est-Elle Chrétienne?," Le Grand Continent, April 4, 2021, https://legra ndcontinent.eu/fr/2018/10/19/le-religieux-sauvera-leurope/

15 "Conference on the Future of Europe," Conference on the Future of Europe, accessed April 23, 2022, https://futureu.europa.eu/?locale=en

16 "Conference on the Future of Europe: What Worked, What Now, What next?," Welcome to EPC – European Policy Centre, accessed April 23, 2022, https://www. epc.eu/en/Publications/Conference-on-the-Future-of-Europe-What-worked-what-n ow-what-next~4609b0

In my view, if Europeans want to discuss what they want to be, they may want to begin by discussing what they are. Profound disagreements between Member States, political parties, and citizens on the nature of the EU are still prevalent, almost seven decades after its founding. It is difficult to debate what Europe should be when it is not very clear what it is; the only way for Europeans to answer these questions is by honestly reflecting on what they were. Now that the Union is going through profound changes including post-pandemic recovery policies and the war in Ukraine, it is the right moment to consider these issues in sufficient depth. It is certain that they will resurface in the future, especially in any debates that discuss enlargement.

For this reason, I would be more interested in joining a Conference on the Past of Europe than one on its Future. Maybe that way we could determine what "Europe" actually represents, and design the best course of action for the future of our continent. A first step could be to increase cultural exchanges among different Member States. While culture and education are largely controlled by national and regional authorities in Europe, this does not mean that more pan-European dialogue in this area is impossible. There have already been attempts to build a European public sphere with the goals of bringing the EU closer to its citizens, and gaining legitimacy in their eyes. This is why programmes including Erasmus exist. A similar effort could be done in the field of culture, history and identity; not with the goal of replacing Member States' powers in these areas, but rather with the intention of increasing understanding on how different nations and social groups use the past to determine their place in Europe. In the past few weeks, we have seen clear differences in the approach Western and Eastern European countries have taken to deal with Russia's invasion of Ukraine. Their different memories of the past have consequences in the present. Better dialogue and exchange of views are needed at every level of society to build a more inclusive and cohesive Union.

Bibliography

Amato, Giuliano. The History of the European Union. Constructing Utopia. Oxford: Hart Publishing, 2019.

Anderson Benedict R. Imagined Communities: Reflections on the Origin and Spread of Nationalism. London: Verso, 2016.

Barigazzi, Jacopo. "Slovenian, Croatian Leaders Accuse Tajani of 'Historical Revisionism'." POLITICO. POLITICO, April 18, 2019. https://www.politico.eu/articl e/slovenian-croatian-leaders-accuse-tajani-of-historical-revisionism/

Baume, Maïa de La. "Eu Accused of Trying to Cancel Christmas! Advice on Inclusive Language Dropped after Criticism." POLITICO. POLITICO, December 1, 2021. https://www.politico.eu/article/european-commission-cancel-christmas-inclusive-language-lgbtq/

Chan, TW, Henderson, M, Sironi, M, Kawalerowicz, J. Understanding the social and cultural bases of Brexit. Br J Sociol. 2020; 71: 830- 851. https://doi.org/10.1111/1468-4446.12790

"Conference on the Future of Europe." Conference on the Future of Europe. Accessed April 23, 2022. https://futureu.europa.eu/?locale=en

"Conference on the Future of Europe: What Worked, What Now, What next?" Welcome to EPC – European Policy Centre. Accessed April 23, 2022. https://www.epc.eu/en/Publications/Conference-on-the-Future-of-Europe-What-worked-what-now-what-next~4609b0

France 24. "French Election Year Kicks off with EU Flag Fracas at Paris's Arc De Triomphe." France 24. France 24, January 3, 2022. https://www.france24.com/en/france/20220103-french-election-year-kicks-off-with-eu-flag-fracas-at-paris-landmark

"En Pologne, L'hommage à Karl Marx Suscite L'incompréhension." Courrier international, May 7, 2018. https://www.courrierinternational.com/article/en-pologne-lhommage-karl-marx-suscite-lincomprehension

Humphreys, Joe. "'Take Back Control': Why the Brexit Slogan Resonates across Europe." The Irish Times. The Irish Times, March 19, 2019. https://www.irishtimes.com/culture/take-back-control-why-the-brexit-slogan-resonates-across-europe-1.3824393

Hunnings, Neville March, and Joe Macdonald Hill. The Treaty of Rome Consolidated and the Treaty of Maastricht. London: European Law Centre at Sweet & Maxwell, 1992.

Lähdesmäki, Tuuli. "Founding Myths of EU Europe and the Workings of Power in the EU Heritage and History Initiatives." European Journal of Cultural Studies 22, no. 5–6 (October 2019): 781–98. https://doi.org/10.1177/1367549418755921

Pinard Legry, Agnès, "Faut-il sauver Noël? La vidéo de François-Xavier Bellamy devient virale", Aleteia (15 December 2021), https://fr.aleteia.org/2021/12/17/faut-il-sauver-noel-la-video-de-francois-xavier-bellamy-devient-virale/

"The EU: Made in America." The Economist. The Economist Newspaper. Accessed April 23, 2022. https://www.economist.com/europe/2021/06/17/the-eu-made-in-america

"L'Europe Est-Elle Chrétienne?" Le Grand Continent, April 4, 2021. https://legrandcontinent.eu/fr/2018/10/19/le-religieux-sauvera-leurope/

Snyder, Timothy. "Europe's Dangerous Creation Myth." POLITICO. POLITICO, May 1, 2019. https://www.politico.eu/article/europe-creation-project-myth-history-nation-state/

Verovsek, Peter J. Memory and the Future of Europe: Rupture and Integration in the Wake of Total War. S.l.: MANCHESTER UNIV PRESS, 2022.

Verovsek, Peter J. Collective memory, politics, and the influence of the past: the politics of memory as a research paradigm- Politics, Groups, and Identities, 2016.

A New Bauhaus for the Green Deal: A cultural approach to Europe's recovery

Gabrielle Bernoville

Introduction

> "I want this to be more than an environmental or economic project.
> The European Green Deal must also – and especially – be a new
> cultural project for Europe"
> – Ursula von der Leyen[1]

Seventy years after the Schuman Declaration, *recovery* remains an essential pillar of the European Integration project. In fact, the revival of the European Spirit has guided every European Commission President's political and economic agenda, from the 1966 "Empty Chair" emergency to the 2013 European Sovereign Debt crisis. In the 21st century, *Recovery, Resilience,* and *Reform* continue to form a three-pronged guide for European policymaking.

Through the 2019 Green Deal, the European Union unveiled its vision for becoming the first climate-neutral continent by 2050. Technical and scientific progress, however, have not yet managed to change the overall feeling of powerlessness among European people. Indeed, The climate emergency, as well as the Covid-19 outbreak, are more than solely scientific challenges. Tackling them requires ethics, social justice, and cultural values; it requires Europe to reconsider its approach to climate action. And actively on-boarding European citizens and communities is the first, most crucial step towards succeeding in this mission.

It is with this objective in mind that the European Commission unearthed the German Bauhaus school's ideals as an answer to Europe's multifaceted crisis. In her September 2020 State of the Union address, President Von der Leyen vowed to foster the creation of a European citizenry bound by a shared belief in the promises of the Green Deal.

---

1 European Commission (2021, April 22). *Speech by President von der Leyen at the New European Bauhaus Conference*. European Commission. Retrieved April 13, 2022, from https://ec.europa.eu/commission/presscorner/detail/fr/speech_21_1881

The EU's transformational recovery strategy, framed as the New European Bauhaus (NEB), aims to ensure economic development and innovation while preserving fair and equal transition toward the EU's climate goals.

The NEB's name is inspired by the experience of the 1919 Weimar Republic's Bauhaus school. In a time of war and uncertainty, the Bauhaus school became an influential pioneer in design and architecture, internationally known for its forward-looking ambition to combine functionality with aesthetics. With a similar ambition, the NEB rightly suggests embedding culture and innovation in the broader European socio-political context. For instance, it notes that the renovation of Europe's housing infrastructure – responsible for at least 40 % of all greenhouse gas emissions – should use renewable materials without having to compromise for comfort or attractiveness.

Conceived as an interdisciplinary initiative bridging the world of technology and the world of art, the NEB appears as a fresh transformational approach to complex societal problems. The NEB has certainly raised expectations, but the achievability of this initiative must be soberly assessed. To do so, this essay dissects the EU Recovery Strategy before discussing the three main challenges faced by the NEB. The essay ultimately argues that unless policymakers accept involvement and contributions external to their institutions, the strategy as a whole may fail. It concludes by outlining how the strategy can succeed.

The EU's Clay-Footed Transformational Myth

The NEB emerged at a crucial moment in the EU's recovery and its parallel effort to improve the quality of life for Europeans. Announced as a "human-centered, positive, and tangible" transformational project, it strives to create new "European spaces" of dialogue connecting disciplines, cultures, and generations.

The title of the Commission's transformational strategy is inspired by the success of the historical Bauhaus school in a time of profound transformation. The Staatliches Bauhaus refers to the avant-garde design Gesamtkunstwerk, which was shaped by a handful of modernist craftsmen, artists, and architects in the turmoil that followed World War One. The Weimar-based school gathered prominent international artists in a short-lived interdisciplinary attempt to combine aesthetics and functionality. It promoted new materials like steel and cement to respond to the continent's demographic pressures and economic shifts. Despite this legacy, its modern lineage only received a mild welcome in political spheres.

United in sustainability – Stronger in diversity

As a bridge "between the world of science and technology and the world of art and culture," the NEB complements the EU's climate and recovery policies. The NEB framework comprises an essential cultural dimension, turning culture into a principal driver for its policy objectives.

In practical terms, the NEB aspires to stimulate debates and fund cross-disciplinary green social projects. It aims at providing practical answers to the social question of what modern life in harmony with nature could look like for the European citizenry. The implementation of the NEB revolves around three phases, occurring partly in parallel, that encourage partners to deliver and scale up on green cross-disciplinary actions. The first, Co-Design Phase aspires to gather examples of existing European projects which mirror the NEB principles. It will additionally convene consultations and debates, facilitate high-level roundtables, and designate best practices. The second, Delivery Phase will provide financial support to innovative ideas and environmentally sustainable, socially focused projects through ad hoc calls and programs organized by the Multi-Annual Financial Framework. This strategy leverages and benefits from the digitization megatrend by relying on technological solutions to improve design decisions in terms of resource efficiency. Finally, the third, Dissemination Phase will encourage networking and knowledge-sharing to scale up agreed upon solutions. Ultimately, the NEB will support the emergence of innovation lead markets.

In 2021, this strategy took the shape of best-practice conversations as well as open roundtables gathering designers, architects, artists, digital experts, scientists, entrepreneurs, engineers and students. The NEB launched its five pilot projects covering a wide area of recovery, since materials and energy efficiency, demographics, future-oriented mobility, and resource-efficient digital innovation, are always combined with culture and art. To support this movement and further incentivise the many key players necessary for this strategy to succeed, NEB revealed a seed funding opportunity of 25 million euros.

The policy was enthusiastically welcomed by stakeholders, who sought an opportunity to gear up their pan-European collaborations. It nonetheless fed concerns and criticism, including within cultural sectors. Two years after its announcement and despite political goodwill, the NEB as currently constructed remains difficult to grasp both for its target audiences and the larger public.

While aspiring to generate wide bottom-up innovation and projects, NEB struggled to lift ideas to the standard it set for itself. To generate the long-awaited spillover effects and reconnect the European citizenry on climate targets, the NEB will have to further reflect on its management model, structure, and narrative.

The NEB's Three Main Challenges

Beyond Bureaucracies: Uprooting the NEB

The NEB embodies the very first EU Institutional project to include a co-creation and co-design approach offering fresh spaces for dialogue. It admittedly reflects a political and institutional awareness of the need to reinvent approaches to policymaking in order to face future challenges. Management of the NEB was thus delegated to the more independent Joint Research Center (JRC) body.

Nonetheless, to build trustworthy relationships and human-centric projects, the NEB will have to ingeniously answer underlying controversies and address several hurdles: lack of proper human and financial resources, inclusiveness, accusations of bureaucratic character, and Eurocentrism. Although prominent artistic names have kindly accepted to contribute to its launch through its High-Level Round Tables, the NEB's trademark is still standing on thin ice.

The targets set by the Green Deal are paramount to EU policymaking for the coming three decades. Although the NEB was a supposed cornerstone of this strategy, it would benefit from being further mainstreamed across the EU's existing cultural actions and flagship initiatives. Finally, the NEB would have to prove that its approach utilises strategic institutional communication grounded in collaboration. This initiative would likely be closely monitored by civil society.

Beyond Narratives: Rebranding the NEB

The historical NEB trademark "Chicago, Tel Aviv, Ascona, Dessau, Kaliningrad" enabled it to represent more than its namesake. The Bauhaus stands as an ideal for society-centered creativity projects, reinventing ways of living, and practices. Nonetheless, is the Bauhaus an appropriate reference for today's world? The historical school has been a guide for modernization and serial industrialization in the past century, associated with the belief that it could meet post-war social needs. As the world experiences the emergence of a new paradigm and Industrial Revolution, references to 1920s Bauhaus may appear slightly dated. The lack of diversity of the historically male-dominated school, as well as its lack of ecological consideration, bolsters these criticisms.

This reference which is niche for the vast majority of Europeans might not be ideal for EU Member States' understanding of the NEB, and feeling of belonging to its mission. Future scaling up and inclusion in EU external affairs may require the NEB to rebrand itself in order to maximize the avenues for international cooperation. As an example, the curators of the 100th Bauhaus anniversary exhibition preferred the "Bauhaus Imaginista" headline.

Beyond Procedures: Empowering the NEB

Addressing EU recovery challenges will require the mass mobilization and active contribution of European citizens. In this context, the NEB intends to reinforce its democratic roots by offering stakeholders and citizens the opportunity to "co-design" the program during bottom-up "conversations". Furthermore, the NEB is testing a community empowerment process to increase social participation, as well as to grow understanding and trust in its strategy.

As sketched in its toolkit, the Commission intends, through these conversations, to gather insights and recommendations which will nurture the project's next steps. Similarly, it garners the vision of advanced thinkers and practitioners coming together as NEB ambassadors and engaging their communities in high-level roundtables. The compilation of 30+ cross-sectorial projects and the NEB Ambassadors' visions will enable the NEB team to transcend its project's contested genealogy and instill the NEB's spirit among a wider range of sectors, thereby scaling up the project throughout Europe. The "co-design" phase is being implemented through regular seminars aiming at engaging citizens and growing the momentum of the movement. The "New European Bauhaus Prize" pilot projects and the seed grant programs were announced in the fall of 2021.

Encouraging Europeans to drift away from certain sectors in order to generate spaces for innovation and teach "green skills" remains a work in progress which will require methodical development and evolution.

Unleashing the potential of the NEB – Criteria for success

1. Engage with Europe's narratives and responsibilities

In creating these new public spaces for intellectual exchange and climate-related innovation, the NEB needs to clarify ownership and define responsibilities with its target audiences. The Institutional realm in which the movement was conceived does not escape asymmetries in institutional development. Greater effort and increased investment should be placed into sustainable, scalable cooperation between European institutions and their target audiences.

EU policymakers should be more clearly involved while cultural and socio-entrepreneurial professionals should be consulted at each step of the process design. In doing so, the NEB would further mainstream culture in broader social and political contexts, and re-engage with historical European relations both within and beyond its borders. The question of Fairness and Inclusion at the core of this project should be more carefully reflected in the EU's actions.

2. Enabling Environment: Finance, Data and Research

Spearheading a global, fair recovery depends on engaging the NEB's target audience through the creation of greater opportunities for innovation as well as for market-orientated investment opportunities for the NEB targeted audience. These opportunities guaranteed by public funding should be accessible to micro, small and medium-sized enterprises (MSMEs), and in particular, to women and young people. The informality of certain cultural sectors has prevented a comprehensive understanding of gender participation and equality, making this point especially important. More data to assess the role of culture on sustainable development is essential.

Enabling targeted sectors to take over NEB objectives additionally requires allocation of whatever financial support may be necessary for industry professionals to invest in innovation. Unrestricted funding and a long-term sectoral approach should be favored to guide the aforementioned target sectors on the NEB pathway.

Finally, the NEB's targeted audiences – and primarily cultural and creative Sectors – should be further included in the Recovery and Resilience Facility (EU recovery instrument), National Recovery and Resilience Plans (RRPs), and should benefit from National and EU reforms such as improving the status of the artists or developing legislative frameworks to better address the sector's needs. Similarly, target audiences should be prioritized for national and EU investment to aid in the green and digital transition cultural and creative sectors, the acquisition of digital skills, and the improvement of energy efficiency in cultural sites.

3. Invest in awareness-raising action and foster broader understanding

The NEB bases its legitimacy on its people-centered approach. It has been well integrated into EU institutions through assemblies such as the European Parliament's New European Bauhaus Friendship Group. Similarly, it has been hoped that its "practical" approach would result in spillover effects. Indeed, the NEB leads Europe's renovation wave and aims to improve practices and the way all Europeans live by considering public spaces as well as urban and rural areas. Yet many non-state actors underline that this process is still struggling to solidify its democratic roots. Although the design is a widely recognised tool for society building, more investment should be placed in awareness-raising activities to transform this top-down initiative into a bottom-up movement.

The NEB's Achilles heel is rooted in the technicalities of EU jargon and the uneven levels of climate change and sustainability literacy across European citizens. In this context, to create an enabling environment, the European funding instruments should simplify their procedures and language, and be coupled with training support.

Additionally, since the NEB follows a human-centric approach, the EU should launch a communications campaign (titled, for instance, "They are the New Bauhaus") featuring creators, project leaders, but also renowned public figures willing to show their support. With 2022 being celebrated as the European Year of Youth, the NEB should develop new programs to strengthen young people's climate change literacy, and invest in tools to devise education activities. Involving young Europeans at the local level is key to the NEB's development. A successful example which is to be further developed was the Commission's Collective Citizen Engagement Call. This initiative involved several cities in cultivating community capacity and leadership in the NEB context. It eventually aims to create citizen collectives and active pressure groups.

4. Embrace Co-Designing and Collaboration

The NEB, handed over to the independent JRC, attests to the EU's desire to avoid bureaucratic policy-making. Unlocking this holistic collaborative process ultimately requires funding local, and regional actions in order to actively account for European people's diverse concerns and way of life. Tangible human resources and further inclusion in existing programs should enable people to actively take action and share the ownership of this policy.

The EU's cultural funding program, Creative Europe has for instance included calls to support sectoral action, to respond to the shared needs of those cultural and creative sectors. Involving these sectors not only requires consultations and open dialogue at the EU and local levels, but also to reconsider artists' working conditions and status to better empower them in the long term. The NEB additionally seeks to tap into the research and innovation community.

Indeed research and innovation programmes directly contribute to development in areas such as building materials, building efficiency, circularity, bio-based materials, social innovation, etc. Therefore, further funds and support to scientists, scholars and researchers should be expected.

In this attempt, the NEB is backed up by the European Institute of Innovation and Technology (EIT) and its community of more than 2000 partners to increase the visibility of this initiative. Through the EIT, the NEB is able to provide activities such as business-skill education programmes or acceleration of start-ups and business development services. However, if these activities receive a high degree of visibility through business competitions or prize money for start-ups, the NEB's focus should also be extended to respond to the needs of innovators and researchers regarding education resources, support and status. The NEB should avoid duplicating the role and work of the EIT, and rather seek to complement it. For instance, through mobilizing citizens to design projects which mirror entrepreneurs' and innovators' expectations in specific sectors.

5. Gear Up the International Dimension of the NEB

While the NEB has been designed as an EU transformational and Recovery policy only, there are calls for a reset of the NEB international dimension based on more equitable terms and shared values. To date, the NEB has received little recognition from external experts and the EU's international partnerships. Although it intends to tackle global challenges, the NEB has no direct ties with bottom-up movements at the international level.

To build on its internal legitimacy, the NEB should be earmarked in all EU external policies and actions. Perhaps we should also consider how International NEB relations (particularly, relating to AU-EU joint-climate action and the EU 10 strategic partnerships AU-EU) can benefit from preparations for, and participation in, UNESCO's MONDIACULT 2022. Adding to this conceptual consideration, it would be favored to involve all the entities within EU institutions including EU Delegations in NEB known as "TeamEurope". EUNIC Cluster, national institutes and EU Delegations could have been more involved in the awareness-raising and delivery of the NEB phases. In many cases globally, they are key actors in strengthening local infrastructure and in supporting visibility for EU actions.

The NEB should support more international, diverse and inclusive projects, especially with its neighboring countries. The EU recovery strategy should further encourage access to market-orientated investment opportunities for international micro, small and medium enterprises (MSMEs). In practical terms, one could imagine an NEB international pilot project between EEAS and INTPA, providing funding for people-centered sustainable projects and focussing on impact rather than outputs.

Conclusion

The hurdles and obstacles faced in delivering the New European Bauhaus illustrate the complexity of attuning EU Recovery to the Green Deal Climate target. The multifaceted operational and conceptual obstacles raise concerns regarding the sustainability and agency of this movement. The institutional attempts to design a fair and accessible green and social recovery may lack enforcement mechanisms, clear democratic backing, and readable objectives. While the NEB clearly encapsulates the Commission's ambitions to gear up their activity even for incredibly complex initiatives, it also represents the EU's expectation-capacity gap and democratic deficit.

The recommendations put forward in this chapter call on unveiling the potential of this transformational EU strategy while refreshing the ideals of the Bauhaus school. Should the NEB be developed further, it would allow a substantial step towards advancing a fair recovery, with the potential to benefit Europe as well as its partners and neighbors.

Bibliography

European Commission. (2021, April 22). Speech by President von der Leyen at the New

European Bauhaus Conference. European Commission. Retrieved March 28, 2022, from

https://ec.europa.eu/commission/presscorner/detail/fr/speech_21_1881

Bauhaus Imaginista (2018). Bauhaus imaginista concept. Bauhaus Imaginista website. Retrieved March 28, 2022, from http://www.bauhaus-imaginista.org/concept.

Bauhaus Imaginista. (2018). In memory of Marion von Osten (1963–2020). Bauhaus Imaginista website. Retrieved March 28, 2022, from http://www.bauhaus-imaginista.org/inmemoriam.

Bason, C., Conway, R., Hill, D. and Mazzucato, M. (2021). A New Bauhaus for a Green Deal. UCL London Website. Retrieved March 28, 2022, from https://www.ucl.ac.uk/bartlett/public-purpose/publications/2021/jan/new-bauhaus-green-deal.

Culture Action Europe. (2020). New European Bauhaus: a promising intention and a much-needed open debate. Culture Action Europe website. Retrieved March 28, 2022, from: https://cultureactioneurope.org/news/new-european-bauhaus-a-promising-intention-and-a-much-needed-open-debate/.

European Commission. (2021). New European Bauhaus: Commission launches design phase. European Commission website. Retrieved March 28, 2022, from: https://ec.europa.eu/commission/presscorner/detail/en/IP_21_111.

European Commission. (2020). The New European Bauhaus. European Commission website Retrieved March 28, 2022, from: https://europa.eu/new-european-bauhaus/index_en.

European Commission. (2021). The New European Bauhaus explained. European Commission website. Retrieved March 28, 2022, from: https://europa.eu/new-european-bauhaus/system/files/2021-01/New-European-Bauhaus-Explained.pdf.

European Commission. (2021). High-level roundtable visions. European Commission website. Retrieved March 28, 2022, from: https://europa.eu/new-european-bauhaus/high-level-roundtable-visions_en.

European Commission. (2020). State of the Union Address by President von der Leyen at the European Parliament Plenary. European Commission website. Retrieved March 28, 2022 from: https://ec.europa.eu/commission/presscorner/detail/en/SPEECH_20_1655.

European Cultural Foundation. (2020). ECF and the New European Bauhaus: The Spirit of Renewal. European Cultural Foundation website. Retrieved March 28, 2022 from: https://culturalfoundation.eu/stories/ecf-and-the-new-european-bauhaus.

European Parliament. (2021). Question for written answer E-000703/2021 Subject: Funding the New European Bauhaus project. European Parliament Website. Retrieved March 28, 2022 from: https://www.europarl.europa.eu/doceo/document/E-9-2021-000703_EN.html.

Impakter. (2021). The New European Bauhaus: Combining Art and Science to a Sustainable End", Impakter website. Retrieved March 28, 2022 from: https://impakter.com/the-new-european-bauhaus-combining-art-and-science-to-a-sustainable-end/.

International Union of Property Owners (2021). The New European Bauhaus: an idealistic or realistic initiative?. UIPI Website. Retrieved March 28, 2022 from: https://www.uipi.com/the-new-european-bauhaus-an-idealistic-or-realistic-initiative/.

Institute of Design. (n.d.). The New Bauhaus. Institute of Design Website. Retrieved March 28, 2022 from: https://id.iit.edu/new-bauhaus/.

Lecole du Design. (2020). Staatliche bauhaus cent pour cent 1919–2019. Lecole du design website. Retrieved March 28, 2022 from: https://www.lecolededesign.com/actualites/staatliche-bauhaus-cent-pour-cent-1919-2019-3337.

Medium. (2021). Thoughts on a New European Bauhaus. Medium website. Retrieved March 28, 2022: https://medium.com/dark-matter-and-trojan-horses/thoughts-on-a-new-european-bauhaus-3aaeccbe9bea.

The EU's New Forest Strategy: Taking advantage of this watershed moment

Bryan Bayne

Introduction

In July 2021, the European Commission published its Forest Strategy for 2030 after a period of open consultation. Even though the document represented a major policy shift for the EU, it made very few headlines and went by mostly unnoticed. This essay aims to analyze the Forest Strategy in light of the EU's ambitious climate goals. Its main argument is that it represents a watershed moment for the EU as it tries to harmonize forest policies and align them to the EU's climate goals, but it also faces obstacles in the form of member-state resistance.

This essay is divided into four parts. First, it discusses policy fragmentation and the role of harmonizing documents like Forest Strategies. Secondly, it analyzes the 2013 Forest Strategy, arguing that the failure of that strategy in achieving its stated goals combined with increased pressure to address the environmental crisis has led to the development of the new Forest Strategy for 2030. Subsequently, this essay discusses whether the new Strategy can tackle the issue of policy fragmentation. Finally, it discusses the main challenge that the new Strategy faces: Member State resistance.

Why Policy Integration Matters

European forests provide a range of forest ecosystem services, from the supplying of tinder products to climate change adaptation and recreational or cultural benefits. Although these benefits occur at global, regional, and local levels, the capacity to deliver forest ecosystem services is generally determined by local management regimes.[1] The European Union has hith-

---

1 Carsten Mann, Lasse Loft, Mónica Hernández-Morcillo. "Assessing forest governance innovations in Europe: Needs, challenges and ways forward for sustainable forest ecosystem provisions," *Ecosystem Services 52* (2021).

erto had very little say in forest policy because it is not one of its policy competencies, as established in the treaties of the European Union and European law, resulting in a myriad of uncoordinated practices throughout the EU. However, as pressure to address the climate crisis grows, so does the incentive to devise coordinated EU-wide approaches to forest policy.

Before the EU Commission published its new Forest Strategy for 2030, most policies and regulations concerning forestry had been enacted within the framework of related policy areas, such as biodiversity, climate change, agriculture, and energy. Thus, although the EU has published Forest Strategies for a long time, one could expect to find forest regulations within the Common Agriculture Policy or the Habitats and Birds Directive rather than an overarching forest policy document.

However, forest policy scholars have pointed out that such fragmentation leads to goal conflicts: each policy area has its own separate goals and decision-makers must prioritize some over the others.[2] For example, policies to foster regional development and climate change mitigation under the EU Rural Development Regulation contradict the biodiversity conservation policies under the EU Habitats and Birds Directive.[3] Therefore, scholars have long advocated for a coordinated EU approach that is more legally binding than previous efforts.

Scholars are increasingly recognizing policy integration as a fundamental principle to achieving sustainable development. Integration of sustainable use of natural resources and conservation is considered a must for societies that strive for enhanced sustainability. Policy integration aims to synergize different policies to achieve a larger goal. For instance, subsidies for using carbon-neutral wood for furniture could be complemented with industry regulations that make the production process itself cleaner and more energy-efficient. However, natural resource policy making remains characterized by struggles among competing policy sectors.[4]

---

2 Peter Mayer, "Preface," in *European Forest Governance: Issues at Stake and the Way Forward*, 9.
3 Metodi Sotirov and Sabine Storch. "Resilience through policy integration in Europe? Domestic forest policy changes as response to absorb pressure to integrate biodiversity conservation, bioenergy use and climate protection in France, Germany, the Netherlands and Sweden," *Land Use Policy* 79 (2018).
4 Ibid.

The EU has previously attempted to address this criticism with two other Forest Strategies. The first one, adopted in late 1998,[5] had limited impact because it failed to garner sufficient political traction—it did not even attempt to coordinate different policy areas and dealt mostly with rural development.[6] The second Strategy, adopted in 2013, was much more relevant, as it sought to harmonize forest policies and establish some coherence. Yet for the most part, this second strategy failed to solve policy fragmentation. The new Forest Strategy for 2030 was developed partially as a response to its predecessor, the 2013 Strategy. For this reason, it would also advocate for the EU to play a greater role in forest policy and, consequently, be much more controversial than any previous initiatives.

The 2013 Forest Strategy: Too modest

The EU Commission published its second Forest Strategy in 2013, after high-level consultations with forest policy experts. It sought to address their criticism and establish an EU-wide strategy, coordinating policy goals from different policy areas.[7] Nevertheless, the consensus is that this document was too modest to achieve its goals. Despite the explicit objective to formulate a more coherent policy, forest policy remained fragmented across policy areas and EU initiatives still were not legally binding.[8]

An analysis of 36 EU policy documents related to forests, including the 2013 Forest Strategy, has shown that policy fragmentation remains a salient issue. Researchers Jerbelle Elomina and Helga Pützl identified nine competing forest policy frames, which range from *forests as "providers of wood and non-wood products"* and *"contributors to the bioeconomy"* to *"climate change solution"* and *"sustain socio-cultural well-being."* EU documents had not settled on a unified position for the role of forests nor weighed the tradeoffs from different policy frames. More importantly, the 2013 Forest Strategy was deemed to only "address a limited number of policy objec-

---

5 Council of the European Union. Council Resolution of 15 December 1998 on a forestry strategy for the European Union. Document 31999Y0226(01), 1998. https://eur-lex.europa.eu/legal-content/EN/TXT/?uri=CELEX:31999Y0226(01).
6 Filip Aggestam and Helga Pützl. "Coordinating the Uncoordinated: The EU Forest Strategy," *Forests 9*, 2018
7 Ibid.
8 Jerbelle Elomina and Helga Pützl. "How are forests framed? An analysis of EU forest policy," *Forest Policy and Economics 127* (2021).

tives and not fundamentally address or even try to resolve the tradeoffs generated by various forest-related documents."[9]

Indeed, the 2013 Forest Strategy had four guiding principles: sustainable forest management (SFM),[10] the multifunctional role of forests, resource efficiency, and global forest responsibility. The aforementioned study found that the multifunctional role of forests scarcely featured in forest-related policy documents because it was ambiguous and often left to be defined at the local level. On the other hand, SFM was not only a core principle but also the linchpin of both main stated objectives: first, to ensure all European forests are managed according to SFM principles, and secondly, to promote SFM at a global level.

SFM and resource efficiency are more closely related to the two most dominant frames in policy documents: the provision of wood and non-wood products (i.e., timber production), and contribution to the bio-economy. These are much more in line with the traditional use of forests because they value forests for the tangible goods that they can provide.[11] The focus on traditional economic goals has drawn harsh criticism from environmental groups. They claimed the Strategy "had no teeth" and did not address climate concerns properly. They also strongly criticized the lack of performance targets and an action plan.[12]

The result was that despite attempts to craft a more holistic approach, the 2013 Strategy retained a narrow perspective of what can be considered "forest-related policy." It did not consider the full forest value chain: several policy instruments that generate significant costs for forest-based industries and many EU policy objectives that affect the forest value chain were not included in the Strategy. The 2013 Strategy also failed to adequately coordinate those policy objectives that were included, and it lacked a dominant steering instrument.

In sum, there are three reasons the 2013 Strategy failed. First, it did not establish clearly defined parameters about what makes a policy domain

---

9 Ibid.
10 There are several ways to define SFM practices. The 2013 Forest Strategy defined them as: "using forests and forest land in a way, and at a rate, that maintains their biodiversity, productivity, regeneration capacity, vitality and their potential to fulfil, now and in the future, relevant ecological, economic and social functions, at local, national, and global levels, and that does not cause damage to other ecosystems."
European Commission, A New EU Forest Strategy: for forests and the forest-based sector, 2013, page 3.
11 Jerbelle Elomina and Helga Pützl. "How are forests framed?"
12 David Keating. "EU unveils forest strategy," *Politico*, September 20, 2013.

"forest-relevant." This led it to fail to consider the entire forest value-chain, prioritizing traditional forestry practices over its multifunctional forestry objective. Secondly, it did not directly address the trade-offs generated between various policy instruments already affecting the forest-based sector. Finally, it did not gain sufficient political support.[13]

The New Forest Strategy for 2030: Too ambitious

Therefore, to address the criticism that the 2013 Forest Strategy had failed to tackle the issue of policy fragmentation, the EU Commission initiated an open consultation process in late 2020 to draft a new Forest Strategy. The EU received around 19,000 replies, over 90 % of which came from private citizens voicing their concerns; the remaining were opinions from businesses, NGOs, and government officials. Curiously, nearly 17,000 respondents were Polish citizens, which raised concerns that the consultation might have produced biased or skewed results.[14]

The consultation generally indicated that stakeholders placed great value on forest conservation, biodiversity, and climate change mitigation or adaptation. Polish citizens were also much more likely than other respondents to support prioritizing climate goals in the upcoming Forest Strategy. But the starkest and perhaps most important contrast was related to ranking the statement *"Foster a stronger coordination between national forest policies and the European Green Deal's objectives."* While Polish citizens overwhelmingly rated this as either very important (58 %) or important (20 %), organizations like businesses, NGOs, and governments were much more skeptical. Many rated it as "not important" (25 %) or only slightly important (20 %).

Equally relevant was that the same organizations were also skeptical of the EU's proposal to "harmonize the monitoring of forests"—this would later become a burning issue for the Swedish government.[15] Despite sample bias, the EU has chosen to pursue some objectives that were only

---

13 Filip Aggestam and Helga Pützl. "Coordinating the Uncoordinated."
14 Commission to the European Parliament, the Council, the European Economic and Social Committee and the Committee of the Regions, *Stakeholder Consultation and Evidence Base for the New EU Forest Strategy for 2030*, COM 572 Final, July 2021
15 Ibid.

popular among one demographic: it has added "improved monitoring" as one of the main stated goals of its Forest Strategy for 2030, to name one.[16]

The resulting Strategy published in 2021 is much more ambitious in scope than previous efforts. In contrast with the previous Strategy, its guiding principles are the European Green Deal,[17] the EU 2030 Biodiversity Strategy, and the multifunctional role of forests.[18] While important, guiding principles do not mean much if policy targets and instruments do not correspond to them—the previous Strategy claimed multifunctional forestry as a principle, yet seldom acted on it.

The new Strategy for 2030 features more concrete targets. Its main aim is to achieve the EU's target of reducing greenhouse gas emissions by 55 % in 2030, as per the Fit for 55 package and European Climate Law. The other major targets are: planting 3 billion trees by 2030, encouraging the use of wood according to the cascading principle[19] and fostering larger, healthier, and more diverse forests for carbon storage and sequestration, mitigating air pollution and halting the habitat loss of species.

The Strategy for 2030 also establishes several minor targets. It determines that the EU Commission should develop a standard methodology to quantify the climate benefits of wood construction products and a 2050 roadmap for reducing whole life-cycle emissions in buildings. These are part of the Strategy's focus on the cascading principle and encouraging the use of wood in construction. It also establishes that all primary and old-growth forests in the EU will have to be strictly protected. To do so, it proposed a new law establishing a common monitoring mechanism for the entire EU.

The EU Commission has also moved to define key terms in forest policy but refrained from making any final decisions. The Strategy acknowl-

---

16 European Commission, *Nature and Forest Strategy Factsheet*, FS/21/3670.

17 The European Green Deal is a 2019 initiative to reduce net greenhouse gas emissions by 55 % by 2013, compared to 1990 levels, and to achieve net zero emissions by 2050, while fostering green and sustainable investment. One third of its 1.8 trillion euro budget comes from the EU economic recovery fund enacted during the pandemic, whereas the rest comes from the regular EU budget. For more information, see: European Commission, A European Green Deal, https://ec.europa .eu/info/strategy/priorities-2019-2024/european-green-deal_en.

18 Commission to the European Parliament, the Council, the European Economic and Social Committee and the Committee of the Regions, *New EU Forest Strategy for 2030*, COM 572 Final, July 2021.

19 Under this principle, wood is used in the following order of priorities: 1. Wood-based products, 2. Extending their life service, 3. Re-use, 4. Recycling, 5. Bioenergy, 6. disposal.

edged the need for establishing technical criteria to define "primary" and "old-growth" forests—the definition varies from country to country. But instead of defining the term outright, it established a Working Group that should work alongside the Member States and provide a common definition within a six-month deadline.[20]

Likewise, the Commission has also recognized some of the trade-offs in forest policy but postponed or delegated making decisions. The Strategy simultaneously calls for prioritizing the use of wood for long-lasting products as per the cascading principle and replacing fossil fuels with biomass energy—two contradictory policy goals. While its only concrete solution is asking the Member States to minimize the use of whole trees for bioenergy, it also determines that the Commission must eventually adopt a delegated act specifying how to apply the cascading principle for biomass.

The change in guiding principles, the establishment of better-defined targets, and the recognition that trade-offs exist in forest policymaking have all contributed to the Forest Strategy for 2030's bold proposals. Like the previous document, most measures are voluntary. The EU Commission lays out goals and principles that are meant to harmonize national and EU policy and provides the technical know-how to the Member States to improve policy making. Nevertheless, though the proposals remain voluntary, their scope is unprecedented.

The Commission has explicitly called for the Member States to establish national payment schemes for ecosystem services provided by forest owners. It cites Finland as its main inspiration: the Finnish METSO program pays private forest owners to set aside land for biodiversity. It also suggests that forest owners be compensated for the costs and income foregone by climate change and climate adaptation measures. Additionally, Brussels has encouraged the Member States to adopt carbon farming practices, including the adoption of tradable carbon certificates.

Brussels has stoked even more controversy by telling the Member States how to manage their forests. It says that clear-cutting—the practice of cutting down every tree in an area—should only be used in "duly justified cases," due to concerns that it is detrimental to biodiversity. It has proposed limiting the usage of heavy machinery in forestry and banning

---

20 The Working Group has not met its deadline. It has recently published a report about mapping and assessing primary and old-growth forests in which it considered six different definitions for those terms. See: José Barredo et al. *Mapping and assessment of primary and old-growth forests in Europe*, 2021.

logging during the bird-nesting period. These proposals all have backing from environmental groups but raised eyebrows from the Swedish and Finnish governments. In addition, the Forest Strategy openly advocates for close-to-nature forestry,[21] a system that the Nordics claim is ill-suited for colder climates.[22]

Perhaps the most notable shift, however, is that the European Commission announced it will put forward a proposal for an EU-wide integrated forest monitoring framework. It claims that forest data within the EU is patchy and that it is hard to compare data from different member states. Though the details of this system have not yet been announced, the Strategy for 2030 determines that the EU should oversee the entire system. Data should be collected and reported according to "priority EU policy-relevant topics" such as climate change, biodiversity, health, forest management systems, etc. Unlike previous forest policies developed in Brussels, which were voluntary, this monitoring system would be mandatory: in effect, the Commission is seizing a new competence for itself.

Overall, the Forest Strategy for 2030 seeks to address most of the criticism that had been leveled at past initiatives. It attempts to define ambiguous terms, it recognizes and tries to deal with tradeoffs, and it sets concrete targets and ambitious principles. It even establishes policy coherence as one of its sub-objectives. The Commission has addressed to some degree all three reasons why the previous Strategy had failed.

However, the document still falls flat in many aspects. Although it recognizes policy trade-offs, it does not satisfactorily deal with them nor provide clear directions. It still encourages contradictory policy goals and merely delegates the task of working out some compromise to a future working group. Likewise, it recognizes the need to define ambiguous

---

21 The EU has not yet adopted a definition of close-to-nature forestry, but the term is generally interpreted as emulating how nature manages forests and make forests resemble what they would look like had they never been touched by humans. This often involves only felling fully grown trees, avoiding clear-cutting, and letting nature replace cut trees naturally. For more on close-to-nature forestry, see: Kevin L. O'Hara, What is close-to-nature silviculture in a changing world?, Forestry: An International Journal of Forest Research, Volume 89, Issue 1, January 2016, Pages 1–6, https://doi.org/10.1093/forestry/cpv043,

22 The Nordics argue that close-to-nature forestry is problematic because a recurrent feature of boreal climates is forest fires that quickly clear large areas; Nordic tree species such as pine and birch have evolved to take advantage of these fires and grow in cleared areas. Leaving significant parts of forest untouched could prevent their growth. Dr. Björn Hägglund. "The EU Commission got its Forest Strategy wrong," *EU Observer*, August 27, 2021.

terms but postponed making any final decisions. Although Brussels has gone to greater lengths to consider the entire forest value chain, the Strategy still does not provide a clear definition of what is a "forest-relevant" policy field.

Despite its flaws, the Forest Strategy for 2030 represents a step forward in terms of ambition, goals, and policy integration. Using the European Green Deal as a guiding principle has allowed the EU Commission to craft a much better-focused document that contributes toward meeting the EU's climate targets. Unfortunately, however, the Forest Strategy's ambition has also contributed to its largest obstacle: political opposition from the Member States.

Obstacles to the new Forest Strategy: Political backlash

The Forest Strategy for 2030 faced immediate backlash from the several Member States, such as Germany, Austria, Sweden, and Finland. Their main concern is that Brussels is encroaching on policy domains that had until now been the exclusive preserve of Member States. Some of them, particularly Sweden and Finland, are also concerned that the Strategy threatens their forest sectors.

The staunchest opposition comes from Sweden. Nearly 70 % of Sweden's landmass is covered in forest, the country boasts the world's second-largest forest-products export industry, and—unlike most other EU countries—forestry plays an important role in its economy.[23] Direct and indirect employment from the forest sector is estimated to be around 200.000, or nearly 2 % of all jobs. Despite large-scale, export-oriented production, Swedish forests have consistently grown for nearly a hundred years.[24] The country takes great pride in its "Swedish forestry model," also known as "freedom with responsibility:" most forests are privately owned and there are nearly no governmental regulations or laws dictating how forest owners should manage their forests. Instead, the industry relies on private certification schemes and self-regulation, with the government acting as a mediator and advisor to encourage the adoption of best practices.

---

23 Royal Swedish Academy of Agriculture and Forestry. *Forests and Forestry in Sweden*, 2015.
24 Swedish Wood. *The Forest and Sustainable Forestry*. Accessed March 31, 2022. https://www.swedishwood.com/wood-facts/about-wood/wood-and-sustainability/t he-forest-and-sustainable-forestry/

The prospect of the European Union telling Sweden how to manage its forests has infuriated many Swedish industry representatives and politicians.[25] However, what distinguishes Sweden from other Member States that dislike the Forest Strategy is that in Sweden it has caused a full-blown political crisis. The Swedish Social Democratic government depends on support from the pro-Strategy Green Party and the anti-Strategy Center Party. Both have threatened to call a motion of no-confidence if their wishes are denied, leaving the government on a tightrope. In response, the then-Prime Minister Stefan Löfven appointed his right-hand man Ibrahim Baylan to lead negotiations at the Council of the European Union to water down the Forest Strategy as much as possible and make it palatable to both Green and Center parties.[26]

Sweden and Finland oppose most of the ambitious proposals of the new Forest Strategy. Specifically, they opposed limiting the practice of clear-cutting—on which their industries depend—, the usage of heavy machinery, felling down trees during bird-nesting periods, and the EU monitoring system. They claim that while some practices might look ugly, their industry is advanced enough to employ those techniques in a sustainable and climate-friendly manner. It is not uncommon to find newspaper headlines implying that clear-cutting is good for forests.[27]

Both Nordic nations are skeptical that the European Union is better suited to manage forests than local governments. Efforts to define what constitutes primary and old-growth forests, for example, have met ridicule from some Finnish politicians. One even claimed that "there is no European forest," only "Swedish, Finnish, French, Greek…" forests.[28] Although the Commission claims in the Forest Strategy that it will take local considerations into account,[29] the Nordics fear that the Commission will ignore the needs of boreal forests and formulate policy based on the needs for warmer-climate forests. The Strategy advocates for close-to-nature forestry

---

25 Charlie Duxbury. "Sweden goes to war over its forests," *Politico*, July 27, 2021.
26 "Löfvens 'problemlösare' Ibrahim Baylan avgår," *Svenska Dagbladet*, September 9, 2021.
27 For example, a major national newspaper in Sweden published an article titled "Clear-cutting is needed so that new tall trees can grow" (translation provided by the author of this essay). See: Lars Lundqvist. "DN Debatt: Kalhyggen behövs för att nya höga träd ska växa," *Dagens Nyheter*, October 16, 2021.
28 Frédéric Simon. "Finnish MEP: 'I'm against the power creep in the EU's forest strategy'," *Euractiv*, September 23, 2021.
29 One of the Strategy's principles is "The right tree in the right place and for the right purpose."

and the minimization of clear-cutting,[30] a combination that Sweden claims do not work in colder climates.[31]

The most contentious point, however, is the EU forest monitoring system. Unlike most other proposals, this one is not voluntary. It has faced opposition from 11 Member States, most notably Germany, Austria, Sweden, and Finland. These states have called for rejecting the Forest Strategy outright because it infringes on the principle of subsidiarity. They reject the EU taking over competencies that had been the exclusive preserve of Member States and fear the proposal will only lead to more centralization, ineffective regulations, and administrative burdens.[32] One Finnish politician has gone as far as calling the measure a "power creep.[33]"

The Council of the European Union has already proposed watering down the Forest Strategy for 2030. On the one hand, it welcomed the Commission's desire to promote sustainable wood products and agreed that forests should contribute more to the European Green Deal. On the other hand, it claimed that the Strategy must strike a balance between environmental, social, and economic aspects of forestry and expressed doubt about centralizing policymaking in Brussels. The Council of the EU called for respecting the diversity of forest management practices, a rebuff to the Commission's desire to limit clear-cutting and promote close-to-nature forestry. It also expressed doubt about the monitoring system.[34]

Conclusion

The opposition to the Forest Strategy for 2030 raises the question: is *any* ambitious forest strategy with concrete, legally-binding targets feasible?

---

30 For academic discussion regarding why Sweden has avoided close-to-nature and continuity forestry, see: Iris Maria Hertog et all, "Barriers to expanding continuous cover forestry in Sweden for delivering multiple ecosystem services," *Ecosystem Services*, 2022.

31 Dr. Björn Hägglund. "The EU Commission got its Forest Strategy wrong," *EU Observer*, August 27, 2021.

32 Elena Sánchez Nicolás. "EU diplomats oppose common forest-monitoring rules," *EU Observer*, September 16, 2021.

33 Frédéric Simon. "Finnish MEP: 'I'm against the power creep in the EU's forest strategy',"

34 Council of the EU. "Council adopts conclusions on the new EU forest strategy for 2030." November 15, 2021. Accessed March 31, 2021. https://www.consilium.eur opa.eu/en/press/press-releases/2021/11/15/council-adopts-conclusions-on-the-new -eu-forest-strategy-for-2030/#.

Previous Strategies failed because they lacked targets, enforcement mechanisms, and clear definitions of what constitutes forest-relevant policy. However, even modest efforts to address these issues have stalled in face of fierce Member State opposition.

That is not to say that all measures have been rejected. There has been virtually no opposition to the EU Commission's plan to plant 3 billion trees. Member States have also recognized that forest policy will play a key role in reaching the European Green Deal targets and seem prepared to take environmental considerations into account when writing policy—even if they disagree with Brussels' specific proposals.

This means there is some scope for Brussels to be ambitious with its forest policy. Member States mostly fear centralization and a breach of the principle of subsidiarity—they will defend their exclusive prerogative to set forest policy and see any mandatory actions coming from Brussels as undue encroachment. One solution might be for the EU to adopt Sweden's model of "freedom with responsibility:" leave policy-making mostly to the Member States while the EU sets up several voluntary certification schemes—like Fair Trade—and acts as a mediator for dialogue and the sharing of best practices. Scholars such as Erik Löfmarck[35] and Peter Schlyter[36] have argued that the Swedish model has a high degree of political legitimacy and economic and environmental efficiency.

Indeed, the EU itself has adopted this strategy in other policy areas. In 2021, the Renewable Energy Directive created a Voluntary Scheme[37] program for biofuels, bioliquids, and biomass fuels. This program will work[38] rather like the Swedish forestry model: the EU approves certain private or national certification schemes that ensure products follow environmental and sustainability standards and leaves it up to the Member States how to implement it. This shows that the EU is capable of implementing such strategies to achieve environmental goals while enjoying broad support from the Member States.

---

35 Erik Löfmarck et al, "Freedom with what? Interpretations of "responsibility" in Swedish forest practice," Forest Policy and Economics 75, 2017.

36 Peter Schlyter et al, "Not seeing the forest for the trees? The environmental effectiveness of forest certification in Sweden," Forest Policy and Economics 11, 2019.

37 European Commission, Voluntary Schemes, 2022. Accessed May 24, 2022. https://energy.ec.europa.eu/topics/renewable-energy/bioenergy/voluntary-schemes_en.

38 The EU implemented an 18-month transition period, meaning that the program is not yet operational. Nevertheless, the EU has already approved 13 certification schemes.

This approach would not be popular among environmental groups. It does not deliver any immediate policy change. But it could be the most effective tool for policy integration in the EU's arsenal. Using the European Green Deal as its guiding principle, the EU could create an effective framework for policy integration. It can then nudge the Member States to adopt more coherent policies with voluntary certification schemes, financial incentives such as research grants or Common Agriculture Policy funding, and the provision of technical expertise. After all, the best strategy is the one that delivers results, and the Swedish model has delivered consistently.

Bibliography:

Commission to the European Parliament, the Council, the European Economic and Social Committee and the Committee of the Regions, A New EU Forest Strategy: for forests and the forest-based sector, COM 0659 Final, 2013.

Commission to the European Parliament, the Council, the European Economic and Social Committee and the Committee of the Regions, New EU Forest Strategy for 2030, COM 572 Final, July 2021.

Commission to the European Parliament, the Council, the European Economic and Social Committee and the Committee of the Regions, Stakeholder Consultation and Evidence Base for the New EU Forest Strategy for 2030, COM 572 Final, July 2021

Council of the European Union. Council Resolution of 15 December 1998 on a forestry strategy for the European Union. Document 31999Y0226(01), 1998. https://eur-lex.europa.eu/legal-content/EN/TXT/?uri=CELEX:31999Y0226(01).

Council of the European Union. "Council adopts conclusions on the new EU forest strategy for 2030." November 15, 2021. Accessed March 31, 2021. https://www.consilium.europa.eu/en/press/press-releases/2021/11/15/council-adopts-con clusions-on-the-new-eu-forest-strategy-for-2030/#.

European Commission, Nature and Forest Strategy Factsheet, FS/21/3670.

Aggestam, Filip, and Helga Pützl. "Coordinating the Uncoordinated: The EU Forest Strategy," *Forests 9*, no. 3 (2018): 125.

Barredo, José et al. *Mapping and assessment of primary and old-growth forests in Europe*, EUR 30661 EN, Luxembourg: Publications Office of the European Union, 2021.

Duxbury, Charlie. "Sweden goes to war over its forests," *Politico*, July 27, 2021.

Elomina, Jerbelle, and Helga Pützl. "How are forests framed? An analysis of EU forest policy," *Forest Policy and Economics 127* (2021).

Hägglund, Björn. "The EU Commission got its Forest Strategy wrong," *EU Observer*, August 27, 2021.

Hertog, Iris Maria, Sara Brogaard, and Torsten Krause. "Barriers to expanding continuous cover forestry in Sweden for delivering multiple ecosystem services," Ecosystem Services vol. 53 (2022): 1–13. https://doi.org/10.1016/j.ecoser.2021.10 1392.

Keating, David. "EU unveils forest strategy," *Politico*, September 20, 2013.

Löfmarck, Erik, Ylva Uggla, and Rolf Lidskog. "Freedom with what? Interpretations of "responsibility" in Swedish forest practice." Forest Policy and Economics 75 (2017): 34–40.

Lundqvist, Lars. "DN Debatt: Kalhyggen behövs för att nya höga träd ska växa," *Dagens Nyheter*, October 16, 2021

Mann, Carsten, Lasse Loft, Mónica Hernández-Morcillo. "Assessing forest governance innovations in Europe: Needs, challenges and ways forward for sustainable forest ecosystem provisions," *Ecosystem Services 52* (2021): 1–10.

Mayer, Peter "Preface," in *European Forest Governance: Issues at Stake and the Way Forward,* Joensuu: European Forest Institute, 2013.

Nicolás, Elena Sánchez. "EU diplomats oppose common forest-monitoring rules," *EU Observer*, September 16, 2021.

O'Hara, Kevin L. What is close-to-nature silviculture in a changing world?, Forestry: An International Journal of Forest Research, Volume 89, Issue 1, January 2016, Pages 1–6, https://doi.org/10.1093/forestry/cpv043

Royal Swedish Academy of Agriculture and Forestry. *Forests and Forestry in Sweden,* 2015.

Schlyter, Peter, Ingrid Stjernquist, Karin Bäckstrand. "Not seeing the forest for the trees? The environmental effectiveness of forest certification in Sweden." Forest Policy and Economics 11 (2019): 375–382.

Simon, Frédéric. "Finnish MEP: 'I'm against the power creep in the EU's forest strategy'," *Euractiv*, September 23, 2021.

Sotirov, Metodi and Sabine Storch. "Resilience through policy integration in Europe? Domestic forest policy changes as response to absorb pressure to integrate biodiversity conservation, bioenergy use and climate protection in France, Germany, the Netherlands and Sweden," *Land Use Policy 79* (2018): 977–989.

Svenska Dagbladets TT. "Löfvens 'problemlösare' Ibrahim Baylan avgår," *Svenska Dagbladet*, September 9, 2021. https://www.svd.se/ibrahim-baylan-avgar-wu3 f

Swedish Wood. *The Forest and Sustainable Forestry.* Accessed March 31, 2022. https://www.swedishwood.com/wood-facts/about-wood/wood-and-sustainability/the-forest-and-sustainable-forestry/

Open Societies and Energy Anxiety: Achieving security through diversity

Samuel Blair

Introduction: A Historical Perspective

The European Union faces challenges from within and outside its borders. The migration crisis has put wind in the sails of authoritarian political forces across its Member States, undermining its capacity to protect its core values such as human rights and rule of law. A foreign policy crisis in Eastern Europe–Russia's invasion of Ukraine–has disrupted energy supply and put a temporary damper on Member States' climate ambition.

The EU must plan for a renewable energy economy through the embrace of human rights and immigration. Russia's weaponization of energy demands European renewable energy investments in response. These projects require the hiring and upskilling of construction workers, which can be facilitated through European Employment Services and an increased supply of immigrant labor. The EU should reduce reliance on Russian energy imports and transition to a renewable energy economy in a shorter time horizon by increasing the supply of labor through migrant workers.

A renewable energy economy will also require significantly higher levels of investment in terms of Cohesion Funds than what is currently allocated in the 2021–2027 programming period.[1] The value of these investments, allocated to Germany and other EU Member States, should be reallocated in response to what are arguably more immediate, existential challenges to the EU. A much shorter time horizon is required to transform the European energy sector than what was considered appropriate before Rus-

---

1 The Cohesion Fund was established to strengthen the economic, social and territorial cohesion of the EU in the interest of promoting sustainable development. In the 2014–2020 and 2021–2027 programming periods it provides support to: Investment in the environment, including areas related to sustainable development and energy which present environmental benefits as well as Trans-European infrastructure and technical assistance. Germany received approximately €20 billion in each programming period.

sia's invasion of Ukraine in late February 2022. The capital expenditures for European renewable energy must be facilitated as soon as possible in order to protect European energy independence. This requires an open society capable of using immigration as a tool to transform the European energy sector toward a renewable future, and away from an authoritarian past. The recent UN report from the Intergovernmental Panel on Climate Change (IPCC) states that it is "now or never" to prevent climate change, and that makes the need to accelerate European adoption of renewable energy even more urgent; Europe must rise to the challenge. (United Nations 2022).

Effectively managing risks from climate change is conditional upon the transformation of systems through mitigation investments, accelerated technological innovation and behaviour changes. Per the IPCC Special Report published in April, 2022, "Sustainable development supports, and often enables, the fundamental societal and systems transitions and transformations that help limit global warming to 1.5°C. Such changes facilitate the pursuit of climate-resilient development pathways that achieve ambitious mitigation and adaptation in conjunction with poverty eradication and efforts to reduce inequalities."

Migration crisis as opportunity

Policymaking is a collective exercise facilitated by networks of public and private organisations that exchange resources. Conflicts and crises in the Middle East and North Africa have created the largest number of displaced people since World War Two as of year-end 2020.[2] This has strained the capacity of the EU to coordinate policy between Member States in response to the migration crisis. Refugees have been granted asylum by states such as Jordan, but due to the number of refugees, such practice is unsustainable (Karasapan, 2022). The EU-Turkey deal to limit the flow of migrants and refugees into Greece has broken down amidst the Covid-19 pandemic.[3] Hundreds of thousands of people took a long, difficult path to reach Europe in search for a better life (Palmer, 2022); many have lost

---

2 According to UNHCR, several crises caused 11.2 million people to migrate in 2020, compared to 11.0 million in 2019.
3 Only 2,140 people have been returned from Greece to Turkey under the deal over the past six years. This is partly because Greek courts acknowledged that Turkey is not a safe country. The situation was exacerbated by the Covid-19 pandemic given Turkey refused to receive refugees from Greece since March 2020. Six years

their lives in the process. Pre-existing institutional mechanisms, such as the Dublin Accord which dictates that all asylum seekers are to be resettled in the first E.U state that they reach, are not sufficient in addressing a crisis of such magnitude (Deutsche Welle, 2022). Nations in the heart of the EU have employed border restrictions that place the idea of open European borders into question, shrouding fundamental values of the European Union in uncertainty.[4]

Labour mobility serves as the primary mechanism for resolving asymmetric demand shocks in the Europe Union, and anti-immigration political parties across the continent support policies that would decrease labour mobility to the detriment of economic growth. The establishment of the Schengen Area in 1995 abolished many internal borders within the E.U, as 22 of the 28 nations in the E.U allowed free movement of people crossing from one E.U member-state into another.[5] Countries such as France and Germany that compose the heart of the E.U temporarily reintroduced border controls in response to refugee waves from the Syrian Civil War, using the Schengen Borders Code. France is still using SBC protocols to maintain temporary border controls in response to the Covid-19 pandemic until April 30, 2022.[6] The current refugee crisis from Ukraine caused Estonia to reintroduce temporary border controls to facilitate the entry and reception of people arriving from Ukraine. Le Pen in France is opposed to any European defense effort in response to Russian aggression and wants to reestablish national border controls.

The Schengen agreement is of vital importance to the labor mobility of the greater European economy. Labor mobility is the mechanism that

---

since the deal was implemented, no mass returns have been made from Greece to Turkey.

4 In December 2021, the European Commission proposed reforms of the Schengen Borders Code to increase surveillance and controls over non-EU citizens crossing internal and external borders.

5 On March 26, 1995, Belgium, Germany, France, Luxembourg, the Netherlands, Spain and Portugal signed the Schengen agreement. Today, 22 EU member-states are members of the Schengen Area. The border-free Schengen Area permits free movement to more than 400 million EU citizens, along with non-EU nationals living in the EU or visiting the EU as tourists, exchange students or for business purposes. Free movement oenables every EU citizen to travel, work and live in the EU.

6 According to a 2022 report from the EU Directorate-General for Migration and Home Affairs concerning member-states' notifications of the temporary reintroduction of border control at internal borders pursuant to Article 25 and 28 et seq. of the Schengen Borders Code

labor markets use to improve the allocation of workers to firms, and increased labor mobility allows workers to better capitalize on their specific qualities in addition to firms hiring more productive workers (Borjas, 2012). This context allows for the analysis of migration as a form of human capital investment which increases the macroeconomic efficiency of economies that allow the forces of migration to efficiently allocate workers to firms (Ibid.). The ability of workers to move freely to where they are best suited to work is also crucial for the capacity of economies to overcome demand shocks and restore full employment. In Europe, where labour markets are more rigid than other regions, the maintenance of free movement of labour between the Union's countries helps relieve forces in the continent that limit labour mobility such as the cost of working in a different country where most people speak a different language.

Reallocation of Cohesion Policy Funds

According to the European Labor Authority, "The green agenda is and will continue to have an impact on the demand for skills related to 'green production' or the circular economy".[7] The green agenda is the only viable strategy for European defense within the context of a Russian state intent on seizing European land to further its imperial ambition. According to researchers at German insurer Allianz SE, elimination of European Union reliance on Russian gas imports, "would require additional annual spending of at least 170 billion Euros on renewable-energy production over six years, or about 1.3 % of the bloc's gross domestic product" (Strasburg and Dvorak, 2022). Roughly one-third of the €1,082 billion European budget in 2014–2020 was devoted to cohesion policies or €351.8 billion.[8]

The European Union attempts to achieve convergence to equitable and high standards of living across its Member States through the design of redistribution measures that are meant to incubate an environment favourable to long-term growth. Specifically, this is accomplished by the transference of grants to Member States from the European Union, "to lead to optimum welfare in the long run, because they target investments in the improvement of production factors" (Molle, 1990). Other Member States' Cohesion Policy funding appropriations will also need to be reallo-

---

7 Analysis of shortage and surplus occupations 2021 from January 19, 2022
8 An introduction to EU Cohesion Policy 2014-2020 from June 2014 | European Commission

cated towards the effort to shift the German energy sector towards renewable sources. Such an apportionment is necessary given the shortfall in Cohesion funds allocated to Germany, relative to the estimated funding needs tied to a transition to renewable energy, as per Allianz SE. For comparison, in 2021–2027 EU funds allocated to Cohesion Policy amount to 392 billion Euros. The future of Europe depends upon energy independence from Russia, so reallocation of a part of the 392 billion Euros in 2021–2027 Cohesion Policy funding to 170 billion for Germany's renewable energy transition aligns with the initial goals of Cohesion Policy.

The Partnership Agreement reached on April 19, 2022, between Germany and the European Commission sets the foundation for the allocation of €20 billion across 52 operational programs with priority, "given to strategic investments in energy efficiency and the reduction of carbon emissions to achieve climate neutrality in Germany by 2045", according to the European Commission. Additionally, "the funds will help the workforce and businesses in growing more resilient by supporting investments in upskilling and reskilling to create a climate-neutral, more digital and inclusive society." The 2014–2020 Cohesion Funds allocated to Germany across 32 operational programs focused on reducing CO_2 emissions in all sectors of the economy, utilising labour market potential, increasing social inclusion, and improving educational outcomes in addition to other initiatives that strengthened the competitiveness of German industry. The total allocation from German Cohesion Policy funding for the 2007–2013 period was €26.3 billion. Since the beginning of the 2007–2013 funding period, Cohesion Policy investments helped Germany create 88 000 jobs, and support 5,900 projects in the field of renewable energy.

The most important factor of production within the context of the green agenda is human capital. Per the latest findings of the Intergovernmental Panel on Climate Change (IPCC), the UN Secretary-General insisted that unless governments everywhere reassess their energy policies, the world will become uninhabitable (United Nations, 2022). Given the immediate dual threats of Russian aggression in Ukraine and climate change, European Union Cohesion Policy should be reallocated immediately to direct grant funds toward the European employment services, EURES.

The EURES is a European cooperation network between the European Commission, the European Labour Authority, the national public and other admitted employment services in all the EU countries in addition to Iceland, Liechtenstein, Norway and Switzerland. EURES facilitates the free movement of workers by providing information and employment support services to workers and employers, and by enhancing cooperation and information exchange between its member organizations. According to a EURES analysis of shortage and surplus occupations 2021, this EU institution recommends that demands for labor related to the green agenda "should be integrated into the programming of EURES activities and used by Public Employment Services' staff to advise job seekers on the relative employability of different occupations." Specifically:

- EU and national campaigns, for example, should promote the usefulness of acquiring medium-level vocational qualifications – particularly vocational qualifications associated with construction and engineering.
- Employers should be encouraged to adopt a 'human capital management' approach to staff recruitment and retention. This includes the possibility of recruiting persons who may be under-qualified for the job and upskilling them.
- The European Green Deal, as well as the Recovery and Resilience Facility of the European Commission, definitively stress the importance of skills – not only for the elite on the labour market, <u>but even more so for the more disadvantaged ones" (European Labor Authority, 2022).</u>

The European Cohesion Fund supports only environmental projects as well as Trans-European Transport Networks (European Commission, 2022). These objectives are clearly applicable to the acceleration of Europe's transition to a green energy sector. EU policymakers, from the European Council to the European Parliament, should reevaluate the use of Cohesion funds in order to support the immediate needs of the transition to renewable energy in light of Russia's aggression in Ukraine. The EURES' funding should be bolstered to complement the labor needs of increased spending on renewable energy in Germany through the reallocation of Cohesion Policy funds toward this agency.

Conclusion

The €20 billion allocated for German Cohesion Policy funding through 2021–2027 is partially intended for flood protection, urban mobility initiatives, environmental protection and pollution reduction. However, according to the expert analysis of Allianz SE, the German transition to renewable energy will require €170 billion in investments a year (Wilkes, 2022). Germany, as Europe's largest buyer of Russian energy, should transition away from Russian energy imports in an accelerated time frame through migrant labor and the reallocation of Cohesion funds toward renewable energy investments. This policy will address multiple economic, human rights, and environmental crises simultaneously. Increasing the supply of labor and capital are therefore necessary to accelerate the completion of German renewable energy infrastructure projects and achieve the EU's immediate security objectives.

Bibliography

Borjas, G. J. (2012). *Labor Economics*. Routledge.

Deutsche Welle. (2022, February 1). *Majority seek refugee protections after reaching Germany, report says*. DW.COM. Retrieved April 8, 2022, from https://www.dw.com/en/majority-seek-refugee-protections-after-reaching-germany-report-says/a-60310626

EU Directorate-General for Migration and Home Affairs. (n.d.). *Temporary reintroduction of border control*. Migration and Home Affairs. Retrieved April 8, 2022, from https://ec.europa.eu/home-affairs/policies/schengen-borders-and-visa/schengen-area/temporary-reintroduction-border-control_en

European Commission. (n.d.). *Cohesion fund*. Regional Policy – European Commission. Retrieved April 8, 2022, from https://ec.europa.eu/regional_policy/en/funding/cohesion-fund/

European Labor Authority. (2022, January 19). *Analysis of shortage and surplus occupations 2021: European Labour Authority*. Analysis of shortage and surplus occupations 2021 | European Labour Authority. Retrieved April 8, 2022, from https://www.ela.europa.eu/en/news/analysis-shortage-and-surplus-occupations-2021

International Rescue Committee. (2022, March 18). *What is the EU-turkey deal?* The IRC in the EU. Retrieved April 8, 2022, from https://eu.rescue.org/article/what-eu-turkey-deal

Karasapan, O. (2022, March 9). *Syrian refugees in Jordan: A decade and counting*. Brookings. Retrieved April 8, 2022, from https://www.brookings.edu/blog/future-development/2022/01/27/syrian-refugees-in-jordan-a-decade-and-counting/#:~:text=Of%20Jordan's%20672%2C952%20registered%20refugees,Al%20Mafraq%20(12%20percent).

Molle, W. (1990). *The Economics of European Integration: Theory, practice, policy*. Routledge.

Palmer, A. W. (2022, March 2). *They came to help migrants. now, Europe has turned on them*. The New York Times. Retrieved April 8, 2022, from https://www.nytimes.com/2022/03/02/magazine/greece-migration-ngos.html

Platform for International Cooperation on Undocumented Migrants. (2022, February 16). *The new draft schengen borders code risks leading to more racial and ethnic profiling • picum*. PICUM. Retrieved April 8, 2022, from https://picum.org/the-new-draft-schengen-borders-code-risks-leading-to-more-racial-and-ethnic-profiling/

Rinke, Andreas. "Germany Could End Russian Oil Imports This Year – Scholz." *Reuters*, Thomson Reuters, 8 Apr. 2022, https://www.reuters.com/business/energy/germany-could-end-russian-oil-imports-this-year-scholz-2022-04-08/.

Strasburg, J., & Dvorak, P. (2022, April 4). *Ukraine war drives countries to embrace renewable energy-but not yet*. The Wall Street Journal. Retrieved April 8, 2022, from https://www.wsj.com/articles/oil-gas-russia-renewable-energy-solar-wind-power-europe-11649086062

Taylor, Kira. "EU Confronted with Lack of Skilled Labour to Support Building Renovation Wave." www.euractiv.com. EURACTIV, December 15, 2021. https://www.euractiv.com/section/energy-environment/news/eu-confronted-with-lack-of-skilled-labour-to-support-building-renovation-wave/.

United Nations. (2022, April 4). *UN climate report: It's 'now or never' to limit global warming to 1.5 degrees | | UN news*. United Nations. Retrieved April 8, 2022, from https://news.un.org/en/story/2022/04/1115452

Wilkes, William, and Vanessa Dezem. "Germany Faces Reckoning for Relying on Russia's Cheap Energy." Bloomberg.com. Bloomberg, March 4, 2022. https://www.bloomberg.com/news/articles/2022-03-05/germany-faces-reckoning-for-relying-on-putin-for-cheap-energy.

Externalizing the European Union's Climate Policies: Ensuring the Brussels Effect has an impact

Alexios Simintzis

Introduction

As the world seeks to recover from the Covid-19 pandemic while trying to address social injustice and an accelerating climate crisis, Europe has been nurturing a more global role for itself. It has become a regulatory power-house on a diverse range of issues from data protection, fairer taxation, to sustainability, chemicals, and fairer competition. Between pioneering the much-lauded GDPR and its latest commitment to a 55 % reduction in greenhouse gas emissions (GHG) by 2030, the European Union has established itself as a 'first-mover'.

Despite concerns about stagnating economic growth and exploding unemployment stemming from the pandemic, the EU stood firmly behind its 'European Green Deal,' which it intends to use as an engine for prosperity. In fact, climate goals remained central to the bloc's recovery package and new policy initiatives. The adoption of the European Climate Law in 2021, which enshrines into legislation the climate neutrality objective for 2050 — as well as the intermediate target to reduce greenhouse gas emissions by at least 55 % before 2030 — was just the beginning. To achieve these targets, the Commission published its highly anticipated "Fit-for-55 package," a set of legislative proposals supporting greater action on progress towards its 2030 emission reduction goal.

Critically, this package also comprises the Carbon Border Adjustment Mechanism ('CBAM') and Methane Regulation, two proposals with significant implications for the rest of the world. As a result, international reactions to the package – or at least elements of it – have become more pronounced. Japan has reacted against the expansion of the EU's carbon market (European Trading System; 'ETS') for shipping, while several major trading partners, including the US, China and Russia, are openly worried about the CBAM, accusing the EU of drifting towards protectionism.

This essay will analyse the external dimension of these policies, assess their effectiveness in climate change mitigation, and suggest improvements that can ensure the EU's long-term industrial competitiveness.

The power of attraction of the European Single Market

The Brussels effect

In the global economy, power is typically correlated with the relative size of any given country's internal market.[1] The larger the market of the importing country relative to the exporter's, the more likely the so-called 'Brussels Effect' will occur.[2] The effect notes how, in order to secure access to key markets such as Europe, producers strive to adopt the standards prevailing in those markets. More accurately, the greater the ratio of exports to the jurisdiction relative to sales in the home or third-country markets, the more likely the Brussels Effect will occur. On the other hand, the better the exporter's ability to divert trade to third markets or increase demand on its home market, the less dependent it is on access to the market with strict jurisdiction.[3]

The size of the European market and the EU's attention to creating regulatory standards for the single market gives the EU a degree of hard economic power.[4] In 2019, the EU exported over €3.1 trillion worth of goods and services and imported €2.8 trillion of goods and services, making it the biggest actor on the world trading scene.[5] As the results of the European Neighbourhood Policy (ENP) make clear, many countries wish to build closer relations with the EU, thanks in no small part to its enduring power of attraction that can spur transformation in these economies and societies.

However, this attraction is observable worldwide, not solely among the EU Neighbourhood. As explicitly stated in the EU's Foreign and Security Policy Strategy, the EU "has an interest in shaping global economic and environmental rules".[6] While several companies may be able to divert part

---

1 Daniel W. Drezner, Globalization, Harmonization, and Competition: The Different Pathways to Policy Convergence, 12 J. EuR. PUB. POL'Y 841, 841–859 (2005), p. 843

2 David Vogel & Robert A. Kagan, Introduction to DYNAMICS OF REGULATORY CHANGE: How GLOBALIZATION AFFECTS NATIONAL REGULATORY POLICIES 4–5 (David Vogel & Robert A. Kagan eds., 2004), p.13

3 Anu Bradford, The Brussels Effect, 107 NW. U. L. REV. 1 (2012), p.11.

4 Joseph S. Nye (2021): Soft power: the evolution of a concept, Journal of Political Power, p.9

5 European Commission, Communication Trade Policy Review – An Open, Sustainable and Assertive Trade Policy, 2021, p.5

6 European External Action Service, A Global Strategy for the European Union's Foreign And Security Policy, 2016, p. 15

of their exports elsewhere, only a few are in a position to abandon the EU market altogether and recoup the foregone revenue in other markets. The distinctly high value of market access to the EU explains why many producers are prepared to incur even significant adjustment costs to retain their market access.

The external dimension of the Green Deal

The EU's role as a regulatory powerhouse has led governments around the world to implement EU-inspired policies in their jurisdictions. This trend is encouraged by the European single market's dominant policies – particularly on sustainability and environmental issues – and its important market position.

The Brussels Effect is perhaps best illustrated around the EU's flagship Green Deal for a sustainable future and the 'green diplomacy' that comes with it. The need to adapt to the 2030 emissions targets has generated thirteen pieces of legislation in the European Commission's "Fit-for-55" Package alone. Sectors like transport and construction are being particularly targeted for a sustainability overhaul. Elsewhere, REACH has become a standard-bearer for regulating the global chemicals industry; the Circular Economy Action Plan seeks to address international waste. Moreover, a mix of the new Batteries Regulation and Mandatory Due Diligence requirements is set to govern how lithium and cobalt are extracted in markets like Latin America – through carbon intensity disclosures for minerals extraction before they are used by EU manufacturers in the electric vehicles value chain.

The widespread trend towards an EU-aligned regulation of businesses can also help markets outside of Europe catch up in a global race to a net-zero, 'build back better' recovery. Despite the current economic crisis, efforts have doubled, and expectations have only risen.

The costs associated with the green transition and the need for public funds to help facilitate it, make it challenging for many countries that are still paying for the pandemic. The need to access international capital, therefore, becomes essential. Investment conditions, however, are increasingly linked to how aligned local business conditions and policy standards are to EU sustainability criteria or broader ESG guidelines.

The EU's demand to regulate ESG data rating providers under the second Sustainable Finance Package aims to harmonise the financial sector's currently disjointed transformation. A push for comprehensible, aligned sustainable finance standards, driven by the EU Taxonomy, brings opportunities for corporations to build trust with their local stakeholders across numerous jurisdictions. This impacts many industries – energy, mining, industrials, construction and consumer goods.

This Brussels Effect comes in handy, as the EU is eager to become the leader in climate change mitigation efforts globally. However, as we will see in the upcoming sections, that opportunity should be leveraged and used correctly to generate the expected emissions reductions domestically and abroad as well as guarantee a level playing field between EU companies and third-country corporations. An excessive burden on domestic private actors may be counterproductive for such objectives.

CBAM and Methane Regulation

The case of carbon leakage

As part of the Fit-for-55 Package released in July 2021, the European Commission tabled a proposal for a Carbon Border Adjustment Mechanism (CBAM). This will serve as an essential element of the EU toolbox to meet the climate neutrality objective by 2050, in line with the Paris Agreement, by addressing risks of carbon leakage.

Carbon leakage refers to the situation that may occur if, for reasons of costs related to climate policies, businesses were to transfer production to other countries with laxer emission constraints. Hence, this mechanism is meant to ensure that the emissions reduction efforts of the EU are not offset by increasing emissions outside the bloc through relocation of production or increased imports of carbon-intensive products. Without such a mechanism, carbon leakage could result in an overall increase in global emissions.

Until now, this issue was addressed by free emission allowances under the EU ETS. To safeguard the competitiveness of industries covered by the EU ETS, the production from sectors and sub-sectors deemed to be exposed to a significant risk of carbon leakage have been receiving a higher share of free allowances compared to other industrial installations.

The CBAM will be an alternative to existing mechanisms and would replace them gradually to ensure a smooth transition. Essentially, the Commission's proposal shifts the management of the risk of carbon leakage from the EU ETS to the CBAM while also replicating some features of the ETS.

The proposed product coverage of the CBAM is framed by the sectors and emissions covered by the EU ETS. It builds on the climate logic of the EU ETS, starting with sectors where emissions are the highest in absolute numbers and therefore where it would be most relevant. In its first phase, the mechanism will focus on goods which are at high risk of carbon leakage including cement, iron and steel, aluminium, fertiliser, and electricity. The proposal also ensures that imported products are treated no less favourably than domestic products, by stating that the CBAM should also be assessed based on imported products' actual GHG emissions, as is currently the case with installations covered by the EU ETS, which are subject to a carbon price assessed on their actual emissions.

To this day, however, no national or supra-national jurisdiction has implemented a carbon border adjustment mechanism (CBAM), which would make up for the difference between its domestic carbon price and the carbon price in countries with a lower (or no) carbon price. As carbon prices have skyrocketed recently in the EU and now hover above 75 euros/tonne of CO_2, third-country companies reliant on exports to the EU will be paying close attention to developments in the EU's carbon market to reduce their cost structure, including the carbon content of their products.

Such developments have pushed major EU trading partners to accelerate the introduction of their carbon systems domestically to shield their industries from the upcoming border measures. Russia exports 7.6% of its CBAM-covered products to the EU, occupying a top position in exports of iron, steel and fertilisers with significant exposure to the electricity sector as well. In response to the CBAM, Russian authorities were modelling their new domestic carbon system closely on the EU ETS to ensure its recognition by the EU. It is also expanding efforts to monitor emissions nationwide with a proposed climate bill planned to enter into force in 2023, which will require companies emitting above a certain threshold of GHG to report their emissions output. Similarly, China, Turkey, and the UK have in place or are developing carbon markets, reflecting the functioning and price signals of the EU ETS.

Currently under negotiations between the European Parliament and the Member States, the CBAM – if adopted – would be the first supranational carbon system worldwide.

The case of methane leakage

Methane is a powerful GHG, second only to CO_2 in its overall contribution to climate change and responsible for about a third of current climate warming. The European Commission recognised that actions to tackle methane emissions need to take place at the international level. With this perspective, the EU executive reaffirmed its commitments to working together with its energy partners and other key fossil energy importing countries to tackle the issue globally. A result of this energy diplomacy effort was on display at COP26 in Glasgow; the EU, USA, and more than 100 countries joined the Global Methane Pledge, a commitment to reduce global methane emissions by 30 % by 2030 from 2020 levels. Further, the International Methane Emissions Observatory (IMEO) will play an important role to increase transparency on global energy sector methane emissions.

The largest share of energy-related methane emissions stems from the oil and gas value chain. While the transportation or liquefaction of natural gas can induce undesired, fugitive methane leakages, on the production side it mainly lies in the deliberate flaring or venting of natural gas. In some instances, natural gas is extracted as a by-product of oil or coal in associated gas fields. If the appropriate infrastructure is not in place (e.g. compression equipment, transmission pipelines) close to the field, then companies often find themselves in a situation where the least costly solution is to flare or vent the gas instead of selling it to the market. Oil has always been a more lucrative and easily transportable commodity with no need for significant infrastructure. As such, companies often neglect the value of gas or just prefer not to invest in the development of expensive infrastructure to market that natural gas. As a result, a relatively controversial need arises – considering the energy transition: to adopt regulations that incentivise the exploitation of natural gas extracted.

More concretely, governments may "introduce requirements in the planning stages of projects, directly invest in building new infrastructure or adopt policies that allow spreading of the development costs across multiple firms and end-users."[7] Another cost-efficient way is to impose a tax on methane emissions in the same way various jurisdictions have already done vis-à-vis CO_2. Norway provides a great example whereby methane emissions from offshore oil and gas activities are covered by an extended carbon tax.[8]

The legislative proposals adopted by the European Commission in December 2021 are from the strategic vision set out in the EU Methane

---

7　IEA, Driving Down Methane Leaks from the Oil and Gas Industry: A regulatory roadmap and toolkit, 2021, p. 8
8　Norwegian Petroleum Directorate, Act 21 December 1990 no 72 relating to tax on discharge of CO2 in the petroleum activities on the continental shelf, section 2.

Strategy of 2020. The strategy first announced the EU executive's intention to curb methane emissions arising from domestic oil & gas production and impose stringent standards on gas imports from third countries. As the largest importer of oil and gas, the EU has leverage to promote energy-related methane emission reductions globally.[9]

Following the publication of the strategy, the European Commission proposed a regulation to concretely address methane emissions from oil, fossil gas and coal sectors as well as biomethane. The objectives of the proposal are clear:

- Improve the accuracy and availability of information on the main sources of methane emissions associated with energy produced and consumed within the EU.
- Ensure effective reduction of methane emissions across the energy supply chain in the EU.
- Improve the availability of information to provide incentives for the reduction of methane emissions related to fossil energy imported to the EU. Given that most methane emissions occur across the value chains outside of the EU, a consistent approach should help yield the best results.

How to optimize the EU's climate policies to reach the desired result

Industrial competitiveness

The European Commission has allowed for 10 years starting in 2026 during which the free allocations of allowances under the EU ETS would be gradually phased out by 10 percentage points each year and the CBAM would be phased in. However, once the phase-out of free allowances is completed, the EU export-oriented industry producing CBAM covered goods[10] would be highly impacted. While exports have not been included in the solutions of CBAM, they still make up a significant percentage of the EU production.

On average, the EU compares favourably to other jurisdictions on carbon intensity, with emissions intensity expected to further decrease in the future. But, failing to address exports results in a great likelihood of carbon leakage. From an environmental standpoint, it is crucial to govern exports

---

9 European Commission, EU Methane Strategy, p. 16
10 See above: iron & steel, aluminium, cement, fertilizers and electricity.

under the CBAM to limit leakage and facilitate the attainment of the EU's emission reduction objectives without jeopardising the European Climate Law.

While the proposed CBAM addresses carbon leakage caused by the relocation of production it does not tackle an increase in emissions due to a loss of competitiveness in export markets; where products with lower carbon content from jurisdictions with more stringent climate regulations cannot compete in global markets and are replaced by more carbon-intensive products from jurisdictions that have less stringent carbon constraints.[11]

In the case of exports, it must be noted that many products that constitute significant EU exports are commodities such as aluminium, which are traded globally in intensely competitive markets. As such, the ability to pass through costs on the global market is limited. This makes it challenging to compete with products that do not have any carbon costs to internalise. Many EU industries are highly export-oriented, not only through a single product but often through entire value chains. Loss of competitiveness in one segment can thus lead to impacts that extend well beyond that single product to a whole value chain. In light of the recent high carbon prices, such costs should be factored in when assessing the competitiveness of an industry.

Climate change mitigation

Academic literature has shown higher leakage rates if exports are not addressed, as it is one of the most efficient features to reduce the leakage ratio.[12] From a climate perspective, including exports into the CBAM reduces global emissions, compared to a system targeting only imports. In line with this, the Commission's Impact Assessment finds that its proposal,

---

11 Andrei Marcu *et al.*, Border Carbon Adjustment in the EU: Treatment of Exports in the CBAM, European Roundtable on Climate Change and Sustainable Transition (ERCST)
12 Frédéric Branger and Philippe Quirion, Would border carbon adjustments prevent carbon leakage and heavy industry competitiveness losses? Insights from a meta-analysis of recent economic studies, Ecological Economics, Vol. 99 (2014), pp. 29–39, p.29

which does not address exports, would be associated with a 6.8 % export market loss.[13]

The European Roundtable on Climate Change and Sustainable Transition (ERCST) surveyed several sectors and concluded that exports are material in terms of their share of total EU production in that sector and that by not addressing exports there is a high likelihood of carbon leakage because of the displacement of EU exports. Eurostat data on EU exports of proposed CBAM production and sectoral production value for 2018 painted the following picture in terms of the share of EU exports relative to production value:

Table 1: Share of EU27 exports of CBAM products to sector-level production value, 2018.
Source: ERCST, Border Carbon Adjustment in the EU: Treatment of Exports in the
CBAM

Sector	EU27 products covered by CBAM exported to non-EU27 countries (Euro) [i]	Sector production value (million Euro) [ii]	Share of EU27 exports of CBAM products, relative to production value (2018), in per cent
Fertilizers	2.968.442.352	20.670	14%
Cement	995.993.943	17.709	6%
Iron and steel	45.306.429.730	210.321	22%
Aluminum	8.968.505.098	50.625	18%

In the fertiliser sector, for instance, exports represent about 14 % of total EU production, but in some of the largest installations, they can represent closer to 50 %. Based on Eurostat data, this translates to an absolute value of about 3 billion Euros in 2018. For this sector, the main export countries are Brazil, the United States, Ukraine, the UK and China, where EU producers compete with producers from the United States, Canada, Russia and North Africa.

Concrete policy recommendations

To safeguard the EU's industrial competitiveness in export markets while genuinely mitigating climate change both domestically and abroad, EU exporters need to benefit from an exemption on the requirement to acquire

---

13 European Commission, Impact Assessment Report, SWD(2021) 643 final, Part 1/2, Figure 15, pp. 65–66

a CBAM certificate. This exemption can also be translated with the maintenance of free allowances for CBAM-covered exports or include a monetary rebate for exporters. Nevertheless, a proper assessment of compliance with World Trade Organisation (WTO) rules would be necessary to ascertain the legality of such export provisions.

Methane regulation: set up mandatory emission reduction mechanisms for gas imports

Concerning methane emissions of the EU's energy imports, the Commission proposes a two-step approach. First, importers of fossil fuels will be required to submit information about how their suppliers perform a measurement, reporting and verification (MRV) of their emissions and how they mitigate those emissions. The Commission will establish two transparency tools that will show the performance and reduction efforts of countries and energy companies across the globe in curbing their methane emissions: a transparency database, where the data reported by importers and EU operators will be made available to the public; and a global monitoring tool to show methane emitting hot-spots inside and outside the EU, using environmental monitoring via satellites.

As a second step, to effectively tackle emissions of imported fossil fuels along the supply chain to Europe, the Commission will engage in a diplomatic dialogue with international partners and review the methane regulation by 2025 to introduce more stringent measures on fossil fuel imports once all data is available.

Policy recommendations

As the largest share of methane emissions footprint from EU gas consumption is estimated to come from upstream emissions in countries supplying gas to the EU like Russia, Norway, Algeria and Azerbaijan, a binding methane performance standard would be required. Such a standard can be defined for the upstream segments of the gas supply chain using an existing methane emissions reporting framework (OGMP 2.0), targets and definitions already developed by industries. This could take the form of a mandatory – rather than voluntary – requirement that all-natural gas sold on the EU internal market meets a benchmark upstream emission intensity value equivalent to 0.2 %. To cover both imported and domestically produced gas, the point of obligation for a methane performance standard would likely apply to EU gas shippers. To incentivize shippers to conform with the performance standard, they would be penalised for the portion of their gas volumes for which the methane emission intensity exceeds the benchmark value.

For the moment, the Commission's legislative proposal seeks to oblige the energy sector to improve the leak detection and repair (LDAR) for EU-based energy installations, with imports exempted from that requirement. Globally, 142 billion cubic meters of natural gas was flared in 2020 – roughly equivalent to the natural gas demand of Central and South America. This resulted in around 265 Mt CO2, nearly 8 Mt of methane (240 Mt CO2-eq) and other GHGs being directly emitted into the atmosphere. Five countries including Russia, Iraq, Iran, the United States and Algeria accounted for more than half of all volumes flared globally in 2020.[14] Considering Europe is the largest regional importer of Russia's natural gas, accounting for nearly 75 % of Russia's total natural gas exports[15], a methane performance standard would resonate significantly with producing companies and help achieve the EU's climate objectives. Even if this could lead to higher volumes shipped to Asia, the European market would not be easily substituted.

Conclusion

As the analysis in this report has shown, badly designed policies may entail significant side-effects on the economic viability of some EU industries while not helping fully attain the climate objectives they are intended to achieve.

Exports from the EU to third countries matter in the context of emissions leakage and its avoidance through the proposed CBAM. European exports constitute a substantial share of overall production in affected sectors, and their continued viability has complex ramifications along the entire value chain of European producers. Because of that, foreign production likely replacing EU exports may result in carbon leakage. A loss of market share by European producers in global markets could therefore increase the average carbon intensity of goods consumed outside the EU. Failure to address a loss of market share of European producers in global

---

14 EIA, Europe is a key destination for Russia's energy exports, 2022.
15 IEA, Flaring Emissions-Analysis, 2021.

markets could thus contribute to emissions leakage and threaten to counteract the objective of decarbonization.

Similarly, the Methane Regulation proposal does not truly or at least successfully deliver the EU's emission reduction efforts as it lacks a mandatory methane intensity performance standard for imports of natural gas. To remedy this, this paper recommends the establishment of procurement standards whereby "large consumers of natural gas may demand a "low-leakage" supply chain as a basis for eligibility to bid or as a performance condition in a contract"[16]. As a result, the competition between gas suppliers would revolve around the methane intensity of their products. With the Carbon Border Adjustment Mechanism being proposed in July 2021 these discussions become all the more relevant.

Compliance with tight methane emissions rules will strengthen the marketability of gas abroad, in particular to environmentally conscious markets such as Europe. An indicative example was last year's rejection of an LNG gas deal by French utility ENGIE with NextDecade. According to the media, the French government pressured ENGIE to put on hold a deal worth $7 billion amid concerns revolving around the environmental footprint of Permian gas. It is widely accepted that "methane emissions harm the credibility of gas today as a transition fuel towards a decarbonized energy system and puts in jeopardy the potential of renewable and decarbonized gases in the longer term" leaving behind stranded assets as a consequence.[17] However, with the current war in Ukraine and the EU's vision to phase out Russian gas imports, it remains to be seen if the "cleanliness" of gas will still be a priority in the short to medium term.

In a nutshell, although being seen as collapsing and against all odds, the EU managed to set an ambitious green agenda that has pushed the world to follow or at least pay close attention. However, to be effective and successful, the Brussels effect is not enough in itself. Close cooperation with trading partners is extremely important as well as avoiding looking narrowly at the climate goals but rather including economic growth and competitiveness arguments. The risk rhetoric of "we are on the brink of irreversible harm" or "climate change is happening" have not shown positive signs so far; the economic arguments must always accompany such policy frameworks.

---

16 IEA, Driving Down Methane Leaks from the Oil and Gas Industry: A regulatory roadmap and toolkit, 2021, p. 32
17 European Commission, Stakeholder meeting on a strategic plan to reduce methane emissions in the energy sector, 20 March 2020.

Bibliography:

Bradford Anu. "The Brussels Effect", Colombia Law School Scholarship Archive, 2012.

Branger Frédéric & Quirion Philippe, "Would border carbon adjustments prevent carbon leakage and heavy industry competitiveness losses? Insights from a meta-analysis of recent economic studies", Ecological Economics, 2014.

Drezner Daniel. "Globalization, Harmonization, and Competition: The Different Pathways to Policy Convergence", Journal of European Public Policy, 2005.

Energy Information Administration. "Europe is a key destination for Russia's energy exports", 2022.

European Commission. "Communication Trade Policy Review – An Open, Sustainable and Assertive Trade Policy", 2021.

European Commission. "EU Methane Strategy", 2016.

European Commission. "Impact Assessment Report, SWD", 2021.

European Commission. "Stakeholder meeting on a strategic plan to reduce methane emissions in the energy sector", 20 March 2020.

European External Action Service. "A Global Strategy for the European Union's Foreign And Security Policy", 2016.

International Energy Agency. "Driving Down Methane Leaks from the Oil and Gas Industry: A regulatory roadmap and toolkit", 2021.

International Energy Agency. "Flaring Emissions-Analysis", 2021.

Marcu Andrei, Mehlin Michael, Cosbey Aaron, Maratou Alexandra. "Border Carbon Adjustment in the EU: Treatment of Exports in the CBAM", European Roundtable on Climate Change and Sustainable Transition, March 2022.

Norwegian Petroleum Directorate. "Act 21 December 1990 no 72 relating to tax on discharge of CO2 in the petroleum activities on the continental shelf", 1990.

Nye Joseph. "Soft power: the evolution of a concept", Journal of Political Power, 2016.

Vogel David & Kagan Robert, "Dynamics of Regulatory Change: How Globalization Affects National Regulatory Policies", 2004.

The Case for Values-Driven Multilateralism Among Democracies: The implications of EU and US relations with China

Lilybell Evergreen

Introduction

This essay will take a focused approach to the European Union's foreign policy and international development strategy, specifically analysing EU-US-China relations and the impacts of each party's increased influence on the environment, human rights, and values of the region. Given that Asia is the home of multiple rising powers and instrumental in achieving environmental targets, an in-depth focus allows consideration of the trajectory of the international system and how the traditional European-US dominance and alliance may evolve.

Firstly, this will address whether China is perceived as a strategic partner or rival to the EU and US, and how the concept of 'strategic autonomy'[1] and an 'Alliance of Democracies'[2] impacts the EU's global strategy and relationship with the US, including consideration of challenges to the liberal international order and consequences for human rights and the environment.

Subsequently, these ideas will be applied to a comparison of the EU's new Global Gateway Strategy[3] and China's Belt and Road Initiative[4] to understand why the EU may need greater multilateral cooperation to remain competitive and strengthen EU values globally. Development influence

---

1 This term originated in the security field and generally refers to an actor's capacity to determine strategy and act independently, although this does not exclude cooperation with other actors if chosen and advantageous.

2 This concept was primarily driven by the US since the early 2000 s. It refers to the idea of gathering the US's democratic allies in Europe and Asia together under the US's leadership in order to respond collectively to China's rise.

3 "Global Gateway", European Commission, December 1, 2021, https://ec.europa.eu/info/strategy/priorities-2019-2024/stronger-europe-world/global-gateway_en

4 "What is China's Belt and Road Initiative (BRI)?" Yu, Jie. & Wallace, Jon, September 13 2021, https://www.chathamhouse.org/2021/09/what-chinas-belt-and-road-initiative-bri

closely links to security, making a wider analysis of influence relevant to consideration of cooperation and conflict.

Furthermore, a comparison of the EU's Indo-Pacific security strategy to that of the US, UK, and Australia through their collective AUKUS deal will highlight why EU security must remain autonomous even with close cooperation. This highlights intra-EU challenges and the changing role of key Western powers due, providing insight into potential conflict with China. The Covid-19 pandemic and Russia's invasion of Ukraine will also impact future strategy, especially due to China's relationship with Russia and neutrality over the Ukraine war.

This essay will ultimately argue that the EU's current global strategy needs strengthening to protect EU values, human rights, and the environment. Close cooperation with the US and other democracies is key to counteracting an aggressive authoritarian rise, but the EU must find internal consensus and use its values to lead a new form of multilateralism rather than being demoted in a bipolar international system dominated by the US and China.

The China Factor: Exploring EU-China and US-China Relations

By investing or increasing security in a region, a state extends its sphere of influence and therefore its relative power. This can quickly become a zero-sum game: if one state increases influence and security, other states become relatively less secure and powerful. In response, these states attempt to increase their security, and negate the first state's original gains; this is the 'security dilemma'[5] which can lead to arms races.

China's rise over the past decades has often been framed in a competitive light, suggesting that a rising state's increased power comes at the expense of existing powers. Given the US's status as the global hegemon and the historical dominance of the transatlantic community, China is often portrayed in the media as their rival.

But how does the EU perceive China? In 2019, the European Commission's EU-China Strategic Outlook labelled China a 'systemic rival and economic competitor' but also a 'cooperation partner', putting into relief

---

5 "Security Dilemma," Wivel, Anders., accessed March 30, 2022, https://www.britan nica.com/topic/security-dilemma

the substantial EU-China differences on good governance, international law, human rights, and sustainability.[6]

Some have called for the EU to reform this strategy by emphasising its values and casting itself as an effective mediator within US-China competition[7]. But views on China differ significantly within the EU. In fact, all EU states believe that China should be defined as a strategic partner or competitor on an *issue-by-issue basis,* except for Greece and Bulgaria who believe China should solely be a strategic partner[8].

For this very reason, there is a consensus that the EU is not ready to deal with China's authoritarian, state-capitalist political and economic systems, and has thus far been unsuccessful at challenging China on human rights issues, like in Hong Kong and Xinjiang, and environmental issues[9]. Indeed, multiple Member States are currently struggling to balance the short-term gain of Chinese investment with their reluctance to become dependent in the long-term, especially as US-China competition increases and the threat of disruption grows for non-aligned states.[10]

There are also concerns about France and Germany dominating how the EU determines its external relations.[11] Such domination could indeed hamper the EU's potential: specific Member States could develop particularly strong relations across different regions, helping the EU expand its influence, and ultimately its ability to challenge China effectively. For example, Poland has a particularly strong relationship with the US, Spain is concerned with China's activity in Latin America, and France perceives the Indo-Pacific as a key arena for influence.[9]

The EU is thus managing a complex relationship with China, simultaneously seeing it as a rival and potential partner, and having to balance a positive-sum economic relationship with the need to avoid dependence and retain a strong focus on core values.

US-China relations on the other hand are characterised as far more competitive, even though the US and China are highly economically in-

6 "On the path to 'strategic autonomy': The EU in an evolving geopolitical environment" Suzana Anghel et al, September 2020, https://www.europarl.europa.eu/Reg Data/etudes/STUD/2020/652096/EPRS_STU(2020)652096_EN.pdf

7 Anghel et al, "On the path to 'strategic autonomy': The EU in an evolving geopolitical environment", 47–48

8 "The new China consensus: How Europe is growing wary of Beijing." Janka Oertel, September 7, 2020. https://ecfr.eu/publication/the_new_china_consensus_ how_europe_is_growing_wary_of_beijing/

9 Oertel, "The new China consensus: How Europe is growing wary of Beijing."

10 Oertel, "The new China consensus: How Europe is growing wary of Beijing."

11 Ibid.

terdependent. Recent policy clashes include China's authoritarian stance toward Taiwan, Xinjiang, and Hong Kong, as well as China's active pursuit of increased international influence.[12]

This directly challenges US hegemony in a zero-sum pursuit of relative power – a challenge that is reflected in the American public's view on China. From the early 2000 s until 2018, Americans were fairly evenly divided on whether China and the US were mostly rivals or partners. In 2019, however, a dramatic 63 % of Americans perceived China as mostly rivals.[13] By 2020, the share of the American public holding negative views on China surpassed 73 %.[14]

China's growing military, technological, and economic influence is perceived by the US public and political elite as disrupting the global balance of power, currently weighted heavily in the US's favour. Like Europe, the US struggles to balance simultaneous cooperation and competition, especially on economic and environmental matters.

Overall, then, US-China relations are more directly competitive than EU-China relations. This puts Europe in a difficult position as its relationship with China is arguably dependent on the state of US-China relations. As a long-standing US ally, Europe would inevitably be drawn into any overt conflict that broke out between the US and China, meaning any conflict would have wide-spreading disruptive consequences on three continents. This would also affect the wider international order and economy as these actors lead the current system and its international institutions. Cooperation may be most beneficial for all three parties, but their differences in values, governance systems, and geopolitical rivalries risk a decline into competition and even conflict.

---

12 "U.S. Perceptions of China in the Pandemic Era and Implications for U.S. Policy." Patricia M. Kim, January 21, 2021. https://carnegieendowment.org/2021/01/2 1/u.s.-perceptions-of-china-in-pandemic-era-and-implications-for-u.s.-policy-pub-8 3684

13 Anghel et al, "On the path to 'strategic autonomy': The EU in an evolving geopolitical environment."

14 Kim, "U.S. Perceptions of China in the Pandemic Era and Implications for U.S. Policy."

The Impact of 'Alliance of Democracies' and 'Strategic Autonomy' on EU and US Global Strategy

In order to ensure that the EU does not merely toe the US line, analysts have argued that it should pursue 'strategic autonomy' – in other words more independent strategies and policies. The aim would not be to act wholly autonomously, but rather to have a greater ability to pursue and defend multilateral cooperation according to the EU's own particular interests.[15] Strategic autonomy is principally discussed in the security context but is relevant to other areas as well; the 2016 EU Global Strategy, for instance, suggested autonomy in other areas including energy.[16] This is of pressing relevance as Europe tries to decouple its energy from Russia following the invasion of Ukraine, and as the Covid-19 pandemic flamed the fires of protectionism abroad.

Within the EU, however, institutions have different stances on strategic autonomy. Not surprisingly, the European Council, which represents the interests of Member State governments, does not fully endorse strategic autonomy beyond defence.[17] Other institutions take a more nuanced perspective. The European Economic and Social Committee argues that the EU should pursue 'strategic capacity'[18] rather than strategic autonomy, arguing that 'autonomy' suggests a distancing from the US that originally sprung from disagreements with the Trump administration.[19] They argue that the EU's values and rules-based democracy keep it closer to the US than China or Russia, and that strategic autonomy would disrupt the basis for the transatlantic partnership, with serious implications for European

---

15 Anghel et al, "On the path to 'strategic autonomy': The EU in an evolving geopolitical environment", 48
16 Anghel et al, "On the path to 'strategic autonomy': The EU in an evolving geopolitical environment", 3
17 Anghel et al, "On the path to 'strategic autonomy': The EU in an evolving geopolitical environment", 4
18 This term differs from 'strategic autonomy' by putting a greater emphasis on the fact that a state should have the capability to act autonomously but does not have to reject cooperation. This term is potentially more acceptable as it removes a sense of a state mistrusting their allies and choosing isolation.
19 "EESC sees EU-US partnership as anchor for democracy, peace and security" European Economic and Social Committee, January 11, 2022 a. https://www.eesc. europa.eu/en/news-media/news/eesc-sees-eu-us-partnership-anchor-democracy-pea ce-and-security

security.[20] The chaotic US withdrawal from Afghanistan, for instance, put into stark relief the EU's reliance on security coordination with the US.

Distancing itself from Washington, then, would be unwise for Brussels, despite the risk of being pulled into the US-China rivalry. Anghel et al argue that a reinforced transatlantic relationship is in fact necessary to protect international law, human rights, and democracy in the face of China's rise, which brings new values and beliefs to challenge the current system of global governance.[21] Indeed, the recent rise of authoritarianism around the world has led to calls from many states for a closer alliance and coordination between democracies with shared values. Anghel et al argue that although these states and the EU bloc should retain 'cooperative autonomy', democracy can potentially only be protected by an 'Alliance for Multilateralism' and that the EU should prioritise the return and strengthening of values-based cooperation.[22]

By acting together, democracies may be able to utilise soft power within trade agreements and international institutions, encouraging other countries to abide by democratic values and governance. This approach is evidenced by the EU's values-based opposition to President Trump's proposal that Russia rejoin an expanded G7.[23] Post-Covid, the EU has also discussed expanded cooperation with countries like India, Japan, and South Korea, especially in fields like the environment and digital world, which often involve values-based considerations, particularly in contrast to China's totalitarian internet governance.[24] Multilateral cooperation among democracies has the potential to lead to new frameworks and governance standards, for instance, the integration of human rights into the areas of cybersecurity and data protection.[25]

Similarly, the Biden administration has called for an 'Alliance of Democracies'. However, this contrasts with an 'Alliance for Multilateralism' in key ways. Biscop argues that this would unite the US' European

---

20 European Economic and Social Committee, "EESC sees EU-US partnership as anchor for democracy, peace and security"

21 Anghel et al, "On the path to 'strategic autonomy': The EU in an evolving geopolitical environment", 1

22 Anghel et al, "On the path to 'strategic autonomy': The EU in an evolving geopolitical environment", 34

23 "EU balks at adding Russia back into G7" Andrea Shalal, June 2, 2020. https://www.reuters.com/article/us-g7-summit-usa-eu-idUSKBN2392AG

24 Anghel et al, "On the path to 'strategic autonomy': The EU in an evolving geopolitical environment", 26

25 Anghel et al, "On the path to 'strategic autonomy': The EU in an evolving geopolitical environment."

and Asian allies for the US' benefit, namely to coordinate a strategy that restrains China's growing influence.[26] Biscop highlights that this would be an alliance not *with* the US and would signal the separation of the international system into two rival blocs.

Cementing a new Cold War would be to the EU's and the wider world's disadvantage, however. It would severely disrupt international economics and governance, causing deep divides and perhaps a global recession. Despite their overall alignment, Europe has different interests from the US, and this level of global division might force the EU to become a secondary actor to the US.[27] This difference in interests is already evident in NATO: the US aims to use NATO to focus on China, but the European Member States still believe NATO should primarily focus on Russia, a view that is only reinforced by Russia's invasion of Ukraine. Furthermore, although China's rise is of concern for the EU, the two powers are not yet engaged in a zero-sum competition.[28]

This raises the important consideration of how a new alliance between democracies would function: if it becomes US-dominated, the alliance will most likely lead to greater competition and conflict with China. It is in the EU's interests to be instrumental in forming any new alliance to ensure that its common agenda balances the US stance with other considerations. Indeed, the EU is cautious about becoming too confrontational with China and other rising powers and should ensure that its close relationship with Washington does not pressure the bloc into a disadvantageous strategy.

Biscop argues that the 'Alliance for Multilateralism' would be more successful than an 'Alliance of Democracies' as it would function as a network rather than as an organisation, and can form ad-hoc coalitions when specific issues arise.[29] As the majority of EU Member States believe that China's status as partner or rival should be decided on an issue-by-issue basis, a network approach may be more successful in encouraging more states to join. Biscop highlights that such a network would be best aimed at influencing China's international policies, acknowledging that its Its domestic policies including human rights abuses are unlikely to

---

26 Anghel et al, "On the path to 'strategic autonomy': The EU in an evolving geopolitical environment", 26
     institute.be/an-alliance-of-democracies-with-the-us-or-for-the-us-2/
27 Biscop, "An Alliance of Democracies: with the US or for the US?"
28 Anghel et al, "On the path to 'strategic autonomy': The EU in an evolving geopolitical environment."
29 Biscop, "An Alliance of Democracies: with the US or for the US?"

be influenced, as previously shown by unsuccessful attempts against the Soviet Union.[30]

Overall, it is clear that the nature of US-China relations will have significance for others within the international system, including the EU. However, the EU is uniquely positioned to use its close relationship with the US to shape its strategy. The US cannot manage the international liberal order alone and Europe does not have the independent power to prevent China from dominating the international order.[31]

To address common issues such as human rights, the environment, and the preservation of global economic order, the US and Europe must cooperate strategically. The EU can hold the essential role of ensuring relations with China remain somewhat cooperative rather than descending into overt zero-sum conflict. The European Economic and Social Committee suggests something to this effect by arguing the EU and US should form a collective alliance with other democracies for the 'cooperative containment' of China, meaning China's interests are respected but there are strong responses to rights violations.[32] The Committee further underscores that this should also act as a mechanism to protect universal rights within the alliance, given that democracy within some EU Member States has become more fragile.[33]

Case Study One on Development Investment: The EU's Global Gateway Strategy versus China's Belt and Road Initiative

Thus far, this essay has established that China exists both as a strategic partner and as a rival to the EU and the US – albeit a more pronounced rivalry with the US – and that a collective network of democracy is necessary to preserve the liberal international order and address issues like human rights and the environmental crisis. Applying these ideas to a comparison

---

30 Biscop, "An Alliance of Democracies: with the US or for the US?"
31 European Economic and Social Committee, "EESC sees EU-US partnership as anchor for democracy, peace and security"
32 Anghel et al, "On the path to 'strategic autonomy': The EU in an evolving geopolitical environment."
33 "A strong transatlantic partnership based on the common values of democracy and the rule of law, key in tackling global challenges and preserving international order (own-initiative opinion)" European Economic and Social Committee, February 25, 2022 b. https://www.eesc.europa.eu/en/our-work/opinions-informati on-reports/opinions/strong-transatlantic-partnership-based-common-values-democ racy-and-rule-law-key-tackling-global-challenges-and

of the EU's new Global Gateway Strategy and China's Belt and Road Initiative will enable a deeper understanding of why strategies are currently insufficiently cooperative and complex to effectively respond to the global environmental crisis and enduring challenges to EU values.

Foreign investment is closely tied to power relations and is often deployed to increase political influence. Fueling development not only facilitates closer diplomatic relationships between states, but also makes trade easier and more efficient. Indeed, infrastructural influence contributes to all four facets of Strange's definition of structural power: control over production, finance and credit, knowledge and ideas, and people's security.[34]

Alongside significant economic growth over the past few decades, foreign investment has aided China's rise to great power status. In 2013, China launched the 'Belt and Road Initiative', an infrastructure plan to create new land and maritime trade routes to further China's political and economic influence while stimulating growth in its central provinces.[35]

It took the EU over eight years to create a rival long-term infrastructure plan, the 'Global Gateway Strategy', which aims to generate €300 billion from public and private sources by 2027 to finance transport, energy, and telecommunications infrastructure projects.[36] This pales in comparison to China's BRI plan, which is estimated to spend approximately $1.2 trillion (~€1.08 trillion) by 2027.[37] Some EU officials and Member States have also criticised the Global Gateway for not including projects that will begin immediately. The BRI, in contrast, has already identified or carried out over thirteen thousand projects, which in turn have impacted an estimated 4.6 billion people, or 61% of the world's population.[38] Lastly, while China can guarantee project investment through its state-owned businesses, the EU must in large part enlist the private sector to support its projects and must therefore work far harder to guarantee investment.[39]

---

34 Giles Mohan, "Chapter 3: Rising Powers" In *International Development in a Changing World*, ed. Theo Papaioannou & Melissa Butcher (London: Bloomsbury Academic), 57.

35 Yu & Wallace, "What is China's Belt and Road Initiative (BRI)?"

36 "EU makes late bid to rival China on the Silk Road." Lau, Stuart., Tamma, Paola., & Posaner, Joshua. November 30, 2021. https://www.politico.eu/article/eu-makes-late-bid-to-rival-china-on-the-silk-road/

37 Lau et al, "EU makes late bid to rival China on the Silk Road."

38 "How Will the Belt and Road Initiative Advance China's Interests?" China Power Team, May 8, 2017. https://chinapower.csis.org/china-belt-and-road-initiative/

39 Anghel et al, "On the path to 'strategic autonomy': The EU in an evolving geopolitical environment."

China has gained a significant geopolitical advantage by acting first and spending more than the EU, a head start that is significant to China's ability to extend its influence in Africa and Asia. However, there are several ways the EU can still press an advantage despite its delayed, and in some ways insufficient response.

China's BRI has been criticised for creating 'debt-dependency' and forming 'data traps' of critical data in some nations, as well as for its lack of transparency and its neglect for environmental concerns.[24] The EU has already noted that it will require partner countries to retain good governance and transparency, and that it will place social and environmental sustainability at the centre of its strategy.[24] Moreover, countries who fear Chinese hegemony, like Myanmar and India, as well as Western countries like Australia, have been cautious about Chinese investment, something the EU could take advantage of and fulfil.[40] The EU is thus well-placed, through the Global Gateway Strategy, to demonstrate a new kind of geopolitical influence by offering an alternative investment relationship to China's.

Nevertheless, as the global power balance shifts in favour of China, the EU must avoid doing too little too late if it wants to retain and grow its global influence. Some competition with China may be inevitable as an investment is a zero-sum scenario: if one actor gains a project, another cannot fulfil the same project.[41] This competition may be exacerbated by the exceedingly advantageous position it puts developing states in: being able to play the West and China off against each other for development investment.

Yet to avoid getting pulled into a damaging rivalry, the EU should seek to turn development investment into a positive-sum scenario wherever it can. If both China and the EU invest in the same location, their projects will mutually benefit from joint infrastructure and social investments. This may prove difficult, however, as it presupposes EU-China alignment on key social and environmental issues.

In sum, to be competitive in the infrastructure investment competition, the EU must work faster and more intentionally, including by devoting more resources to specific projects. This can potentially be achieved through closer cooperation with other democracies. Furthermore, the EU

---

40 China Power Team, "How Will the Belt and Road Initiative Advance China's Interests?"

41 "Nepal and China sign nine agreements" The Kathmandu Post, March 26, 2022. https://kathmandupost.com/national/2022/03/26/nepal-and-china-sign-nine-agreements

must press its advantage over China by ensuring transparency and a values-driven strategy that provides an opportunity to establish forward-looking, environmentally conscious multilateralism.

Case Study Two on Security Strategies: EU and AUKUS Indo-Pacific Strategy

A comparison of EU and US overall Indo-Pacific security strategy can be used to explore internal EU challenges, the changing role of Western powers, and the potential for conflict with Asia. In September 2021, the US, Britain, and Australia announced a joint Indo-Pacific security strategy, AUKUS, on the same day the EU announced their strategy in the same region.[42] This miscommunication, and the fact that the EU was not involved in such a joint strategy, suggests changing priorities among long-term allies. Although this should not be overstated and does not disrupt support for a democratic alliance, it is significant due to the actors' shared regional interests, not to mention the controversial French submarine deal that was scrapped in the process.[43] These shifting alliances can equally be tied back to domestic politics, including a changing US leadership that remains inconsistent in its approach to the EU, Britain's withdrawal from the EU, and Australia's poor record on climate policy.

Changing and unstable alliances due to domestic crises underscores the need for the EU to provide stronger leadership within any democratic alliance to ensure that its values and objectives are not neglected. The EU should also become more internally united to develop a successful Indo-Pacific strategy. The Indo-Pacific is key to global growth as the second-largest EU export destination and home to four of its ten top trading partners.[44] Despite this importance, some Member States do not prioritise the region and there are varying geographic definitions of the Indo-Pacific within the bloc (see Figure 1).

42 "After AUKUS: The uncertain future of American and European cooperation in the Indo-Pacific" Tara Varma, September 22, 2021. https://ecfr.eu/article/after-auk us-the-uncertain-future-of-american-and-european-cooperation-in-the-indo-pacific/

43 Varma, "After AUKUS: The uncertain future of American and European cooperation in the Indo-Pacific"

44 "Moving Closer: European Views on the Indo-Pacific." Frédéric Grare & Manisha Reuter, September 13, 2021. https://ecfr.eu/special/moving-closer-european-views -of-the-indo-pacific/

Figure 1: *Views of the geography of a strategic concept: Where is the Indo-Pacific?[45]*

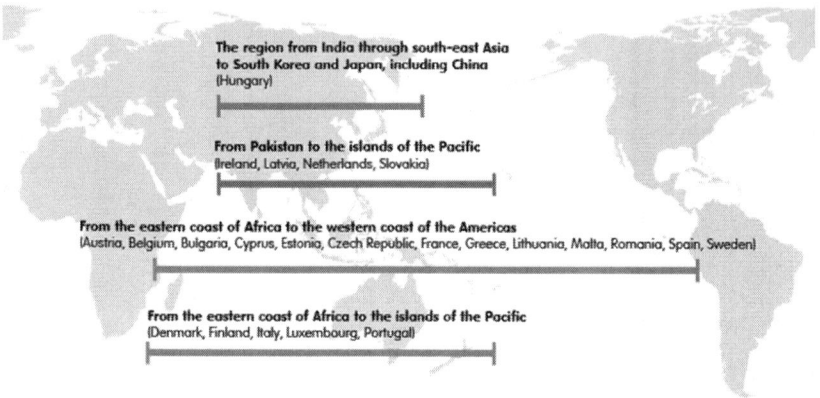

Views of the geography of a strategic concept
Where is the Indo-Pacific?

The region from India through south-east Asia to South Korea and Japan, including China (Hungary)

From Pakistan to the islands of the Pacific (Ireland, Latvia, Netherlands, Slovakia)

From the eastern coast of Africa to the western coast of the Americas (Austria, Belgium, Bulgaria, Cyprus, Estonia, Czech Republic, France, Greece, Lithuania, Malta, Romania, Spain, Sweden)

From the eastern coast of Africa to the islands of the Pacific (Denmark, Finland, Italy, Luxembourg, Portugal)

ECFR · ecfr.eu

Although the diversity of voices is one of the EU's key normative strengths, it is also a disadvantage when forming a coherent strategy, especially compared to allies like the US, Britain, and Australia. Even basic subjects like a region's definition require internal negotiation, often rendering EU decisions slower and more cumbersome. This difference of opinions extends to the purpose of an Indo-Pacific strategy. Eleven Member States see it as pursuing 'European strategic autonomy', eight see it as a method of managing the US alliance, and six see it as directly aligning with and supporting the US.[46] Furthermore, some Member States see an Indo-Pacific strategy as anti-China whereas others believe it is a cooperation opportunity (through ASEAN, for instance).[47]

EU Member States also vary on how they would engage in the Indo-Pacific security strategy. The EU could influence key areas like trade, technology, and maritime security, but most Member States favour non-military activities which would ultimately limit the strategy's effectiveness and sig-

---

45 European Council on Foreign Relations. "Views of the geography of a strategic concept: Where is the Indo-Pacific?" 2016, image. https://ecfr.eu/special/moving-cl oser-european-views-of-the-indo-pacific/

46 Grare & Reuter, "Moving Closer: European Views on the Indo-Pacific."

47 European Economic and Social Committee, "EESC sees EU-US partnership as anchor for democracy, peace and security"

nal a less confrontational approach.[31] AUKUS and the EU's Indo-Pacific security strategy highlight how different the bloc's processes are from those of its allies.

The EU's strength is its joint influence, derived from cooperation and diversity. However, this also provides significant challenges when trying to produce a coherent strategy, especially when Member States have different definitions of a region, different priorities, and different expectations for the strategy in question. In the long run, this risks gradually decreasing the EU's power and influence, both as an independent actor and within a democratic alliance.

Post-pandemic Recovery and Russia's Invasion of Ukraine

The Covid-19 pandemic has led many states to pursue protectionist policies and has caused increasingly negative perceptions of China within the US. There are also signs, however, of growing multilateralism for collective issues like the climate crisis and internet governance. Yet perhaps the key driver of change in the international system post-Covid has been Russia's invasion of Ukraine.

The invasion has prompted a global response from many states, especially democratic ones, issuing economic sanctions, sending military supplies, and seeking alternative energy sources to Russian oil and gas. The crisis has also deepened the cleavage between the West and China, the latter maintaining a neutral position, potentially to avoid sparking greater resistance to Chinese control within Asia.[48]

The invasion of Ukraine also has potential to intensify Europe's interest in gaining global influence and growing its security capabilities. The war escalating into Europe would prove devastating for the EU and US on multiple levels including severe economic impacts, human rights violations, and great concern over conflict leading to the world missing climate tipping points.

Regardless of the war's escalation, the EU has already been forced to seek influence and closer diplomatic ties to ensure its access to the resources it needs.[49] In this search for security, the EU should take care

---

48 "Ukraine is severe test of China's new axis with Russia" Yu, Jie. February 28 2022, https://www.chathamhouse.org/2022/02/ukraine-severe-test-chinas-new-axis-russia

49 Chris Poray, "The Global Gateway, energy security and the Russian invasion of Ukraine" *Encompass*, April, 2022.

to maintain its values-driven strategy and should remain wary of stoking greater competition with China, particularly as its dependence on Asian allies grows. A deterioration of relations with China would be particularly concerning for the environment as the US-China cooperation is key to achieving climate goals.

Conclusion

US-China relations have a profound impact on the EU's strategy and place within the international system. A key challenge is balancing China's status as both strategic partner and rival, and the EU may yet play an important role in ensuring that US-China relations do not descend further towards overt conflict.

But while cooperation is a beneficial outcome for all parties, there are significant barriers to this, especially differences over values, human rights, international law, and governance systems. To continue promoting its values in the face of an ascendant China, the EU and US would benefit from forming a new 'Alliance for Multilateralism', a network of democratic states using soft power to protect the current liberal international order. One key avenue to do so is development financing. A comparison between the EU's Global Gateway Strategy and China's Belt and Road Initiative suggests that there is a need for greater cooperation among democracies to gain influence in different regions through development investment.

The EU's core values are a valuable way to encourage states and the private sector to participate in EU foreign policy strategies, as well as to lead a new, forward-looking multilateralism that avoids negative social and environmental effects. Without multilateral support, however, the EU's sluggish speed and risk-aversion risk conceding the development investment race. The gap between the BRI and Global Gateway Strategy and the lack of a coherent geographic definition for the Indo-Pacific highlight that the EU can remain slow and unfocused on critical issues. Overcoming this will only be possible if the EU manages to somewhat unify its Member States' visions and expectations. These will never be fully synchronous but, without some unity, the bloc risks losing influence as US-China relations come to dominate and destabilise the global community.

To avert this outcome, the EU must also pursue closer cooperation with the US by establishing a leadership role within a network of liberal democracies. This would enable the protection of the liberal international order, including human rights and international law, as well as greater assurance that the climate crisis response will not be disrupted by relations with China deteriorating into overt conflict.

Bibliography:

Anghel, Suzana., Immenkamp, Beatrix., Lazarou, Elena., Saulnier, Jerôme Leon., & Wilson, Alex Benjamin. "On the path to 'strategic autonomy': The EU in an evolving geopolitical environment" *European Parliamentary Research Service*, September 2020. https://www.europarl.europa.eu/RegData/etudes/STUD/2020/6 52096/EPRS_STU(2020)652096_EN.pdf

Biscop, Sven. "An Alliance of Democracies: with the US or for the US?" *EGMONT Royal Institute for International Relations*, July 27, 2020. https://www.egmontinsti tute.be/an-alliance-of-democracies-with-the-us-or-for-the-us-2/

China Power Team. "How Will the Belt and Road Initiative Advance China's Interests?" *China Power*, May 8, 2017. https://chinapower.csis.org/china-belt-and -road-initiative/

European Commission. *Global Gateway.* December 1, 2021. https://ec.europa.eu/inf o/strategy/priorities-2019-2024/stronger-europe-world/global-gateway_en

European Council on Foreign Relations. "Views of the geography of a strategic concept: Where is the Indo-Pacific?" *European Council on Foreign Relations*, 2016, image. https://ecfr.eu/special/moving-closer-european-views-of-the-indo-pacific/

European Economic and Social Committee. *EESC sees EU-US partnership as anchor for democracy, peace and security.* January 11, 2022 a. https://www.eesc.europa.eu/ en/news-media/news/eesc-sees-eu-us-partnership-anchor-democracy-peace-and-se curity

European Economic and Social Committee. *A strong transatlantic partnership based on the common values of democracy and the rule of law, key in tackling global challenges and preserving international order (own-initiative opinion).* February 25, 2022 b. https://www.eesc.europa.eu/en/our-work/opinions-information-reports/o pinions/strong-transatlantic-partnership-based-common-values-democracy-and-r ule-law-key-tackling-global-challenges-and

Grare, Frédéric., & Reuter, Manisha. "Moving Closer: European Views on the Indo-Pacific." *European Council on Foreign Relations*, September 13, 2021. https:// ecfr.eu/special/moving-closer-european-views-of-the-indo-pacific/

Kim, Patricia M. "U.S. Perceptions of China in the Pandemic Era and Implications for U.S. Policy." *Carnegie Endowment for International Peace*, January 21, 2021. https://carnegieendowment.org/2021/01/21/u.s.-perceptions-of-china-in-pandemi c-era-and-implications-for-u.s.-policy-pub-83684

Lau, Stuart., Tamma, Paola., & Posaner, Joshua. "EU makes late bid to rival China on the Silk Road." *Politico*, November 30, 2021. https://www.politico.eu/article/e u-makes-late-bid-to-rival-china-on-the-silk-road/

Mohan, Giles. "Chapter 3: Rising Powers" In *International Development in a Changing World*, edited by Theo Papaioannou, & Melissa Butcher, 49–75. London: Bloomsbury Academic, 2013

Oertel, Janka. "The new China consensus: How Europe is growing wary of Beijing." *European Council on Foreign Relations*, September 7, 2020. https://ecfr.eu/p ublication/the_new_china_consensus_how_europe_is_growing_wary_of_beij ing/

Patton, Susannah., Townshend, Ashley., & Corben, Tom. "AUKUS shows beginnings of US Indo-Pacific strategy" *United States Study Centre*, October 1, 2021. https://www.ussc.edu.au/analysis/aukus-shows-beginnings-of-us-indo-pacific-stra tegy

Poray, Chris. "The Global Gateway, energy security and the Russian invasion of Ukraine" *Encompass*, April, 2022. https://encompass-europe.com/comment/the-g lobal-gateway-energy-security-and-the-russian-invasion-of-ukraine

Shalal, Andrea. "EU balks at adding Russia back into G7" *Reuters*, June 2, 2020. https://www.reuters.com/article/us-g7-summit-usa-eu-idUSKBN2392AG

The Kathmandu Post. "Nepal and China sign nine agreements" *The Kathmandu Post*, March 26, 2022. https://kathmandupost.com/national/2022/03/26/nepal-an d-china-sign-nine-agreements

Varma, Tara. "After AUKUS: The uncertain future of American and European cooperation in the Indo-Pacific" *European Council on Foreign Relations*, September 22, 2021. https://ecfr.eu/article/after-aukus-the-uncertain-future-of-american-and -european-cooperation-in-the-indo-pacific/

Wivel, Anders. "Security Dilemma" *Britannica*, Accessed March 30, 2022. https://w ww.britannica.com/topic/security-dilemma

Yu, Jie. "Ukraine is severe test of China's new axis with Russia" *Chatham House*, February 28 2022. https://www.chathamhouse.org/2022/02/ukraine-severe-test-c hinas-new-axis-russia

Yu, Jie. & Wallace, Jon. "What is China's Belt and Road Initiative (BRI)?" *Chatham House*, September 13 2021. https://www.chathamhouse.org/2021/09/what-chinas -belt-and-road-initiative-bri

Violating the non-refoulement principle: Covid-19 and the erosion of refugee rights

Rasmika Ghosh

Introduction: The non-refoulement principle

In the field of global politics, borders have always played a consequential role, in terms of their symbolic and political significance. They are the literal manifestation of bolstering a national sense of belonging among citizens and excluding elements that threaten the state's security and sovereignty. States are entitled to a significant amount of discretion in terms of regulating and controlling their borders, but as global actors, access to a state's territory does not exist in a legal vacuum.[1] A comprehensive set of rules, guidelines, laws, and treaties govern the movement of people across borders, founded on the principles of the international human rights regime and customary international law.

One of the fundamental principles governing the international framework concerning migration and asylum is the principle of non-refoulement. This principle guarantees that one must not be forced to return to a country where they would face torture, cruel, inhuman or degrading treatment, persecution or any form of irreparable harm. Article 33(1) of the 1951 Refugee Convention relating to the status of refugees prohibits the expulsion or return of refugees to the territories where their life or freedom is threatened on account of their race, religion, nationality, membership of a social group or their political opinion.[2]

The principle of non-refoulement has also been viewed as a principle of customary international law, which implies that even states that are not parties to the 1951 Convention are obligated to abide by the principle. For a rule to be considered as a part of customary international law it must fulfil several criteria. First, consistent state practice and second, *opinio juris*–that is, an understanding among states that the practice in question is obligatory due to the existence of a rule requiring it. This was laid out by

---

1 Richard Plender, *Issues in International Migration Law,* (Leiden, Brill Nijhoff, 2015)
2 1951 Convention relating to the Status of refugees, art. 33(1); Convention relating to the status of Refugees, 1951.

the International Court of Justice in the case of Nicaragua v. United States of America (1984). International human rights law also contains provisions relating to non-refoulement; Article 3 of the Convention Against Torture (CAT) as well as Articles 6 and 7 of the International Covenant on Civil and Political Rights (ICCPR) contain non-refoulement obligations.[3] Thus, it can be observed that states are ethically, legally as well as politically mandated to respect the universal human rights regime and not expose individuals to the risk of torture, cruel treatment, any form of persecution by way of refoulement or expulsion.

Exceptions to the non-refoulement principle

The non-refoulement provision under the 1951 Refugee Convention is not absolute. Article 33(2) of the Convention states that a refugee may be disentitled to the benefit in the two following cases: first, if there are reasonable grounds for regarding them as a danger to the national security of the member state; and second, if their proven criminal antecedents constitute a danger to the community.

The United Nations High Commissioner for Refugees (UNHCR) has further clarified the scope of Article 33(2). With regard to the first exception, it has been stated that, "state practice and the Convention *travaux préparatoires* indicate that criminal offences, without any specific national security implications, are not to be deemed threats to national security, and that national security exceptions to non-refoulement are not appropriate in local or isolated threats to law and order." In the second case, the UNHCR has noted that the criminal history should be grave and should only be taken into consideration when the conviction denotes the "basically criminal, incorrigible nature of the person," which would endanger the community.[4]

Other institutions have supported this view. In the case of Reg. v. Bouchereau (1977), for instance, the European Court of Human Rights (ECtHR) stated that there needs to be a "genuine and sufficiently serious threat" to public policy, affecting the fundamental interests of the host state, in order to consider a person to be a threat to the national security of the state. Similarly, Article 4 of the ICCPR constitutes a general derogation

---

3 Convention Against Torture ("CAT"), art. 3; International Covenant on Civil and Political Rights ("ICCPR"), art. 6, 7.
4 UNHCR, *Note on the Principle of Non Refoulement.* 1997.

clause, which states that in case of a public emergency threatening the life of the nation, the state parties may take measures to the extent strictly required by the exigencies of the situation, derogating from their obligations under the ICCPR.[5]

Covid-19 and the rights of asylum seekers

The Covid-19 Pandemic has brought about epistemic changes in the global political and socio-economic landscape. Containing the spread of the virus required the imposition of social distancing guidelines and restrictions on travel across borders. In light of the same, several Governments adopted restrictive measures curbing migratory flows and consequently, the right to seek asylum. The unforeseen public health emergency was relied upon by states to justify the closure of borders. In fact, the UNHCR estimated that around 167 countries had fully or partially closed their borders, and that at least 57 of them did not make any exceptions for asylum seekers.[6] Some states have also suspended the procedure of accepting and processing asylum requests, citing Covid-19 as the reason for not being able to conduct interviews or process cases.[7] This essay will proceed to explore a few instances illustrating the apathy displayed towards refugees during the pandemic.

Asia

The Rohingya refugees constitute one of the largest displaced populations, fleeing persecution in Myanmar and seeking asylum in the neighbouring states. Cox's Bazaar in Bangladesh is one of the most populous refugee camps housing Rohingyas. The conditions prevailing in such densely populated camps facilitate the rapid transmission of the virus and subject the already vulnerable population to additional health concerns. During the

---

5 ICCPR, art.4.
6 UNHCR, *Beware of long-term damage to human rights and refugee rights from the coronavirus pandemic.* 2020.
7 Akkerman, Mark. "Covid 19 and Border Politics", *www.tni.org.* Transnational Institute. November, 2020.

pandemic, Bangladesh and Malaysia have refused entry to boats carrying Rohingya refugees, citing health concerns.[8]

Malaysian authorities introduced plans to deport and blacklist undocumented foreigners, alongside conducting immigration raids and detentions. The Government stated that the raids constituted a part of their plans to contain the spread of the pandemic.[9] In 2021, Malaysia sent back nationals from Myanmar despite the interim staying order granted by the Malaysian Court.[10]

Europe

Europe has been facing a large influx of refugees fleeing conflict for some time, and several European countries closed off their borders to these vulnerable asylum seekers during the pandemic. The Government of Italy issued a decree stating that "for the entire duration of the health emergency, due to the outbreak of coronavirus, Italian ports cannot be classified as 'safe places' for the landing of people rescued from boats flying a foreign flag."[11] These subjected the asylum seekers to mass fatalities at sea.

Greece resorted to collective expulsion of refugees from within their territories. Asylum seekers were subjected to arbitrary arrests and pushbacks. The government denied access to public healthcare to the asylum seekers, scaled down protections offered to them, and suspended the processing of asylum applications for a period.[12]

In the United Kingdom, the authorities disproportionately resorted to the use of immigration detention in overcrowded and unsanitary detention camps. A refugee camp in Kent was locked down to restrict the asylum seekers from leaving; this not only subjected them to an unsafe

---

8 Lang, Hardin. "COVID-19 and the Other One Percent: An Agenda for the Forcibly Displaced Six Months into the Emergency", www.refugeesinternatio nal.org, 15 July 2020

9 Fishbein, Emily. "Fear and uncertainty for refugees in Malaysia as xenophobia escalates" The New Humanitarian. May 25, 2020, Migration.

10 "Malaysia deports 1,086 Myanmar nationals despite Court order" Al Jazeera, February 23, 2021, https://www.aljazeera.com/news/2021/2/23/malaysia-deports-1 200-people-to-myanmar

11 Tondo, Lorenzo. "Italy declares its own ports 'unsafe' to stop migrants arriving". The Guardian. April 8, 2020

12 Souli, Sarah. "Greece's 'new tactic' of migrant expulsion from deep inside its land borders" The New Humanitarian. October 7, 2020. Migration

sanitary environment but also suspended the processing of their applications.[13]

Reports of violent expulsions displaying absolute indifference towards the health and fundamental rights of asylum seekers were equally recorded in the borders of Croatia.[14]

United States

In March 2020, the United States Centre for Disease Control and Prevention (CDC) issued an order suspending the entry of persons travelling from Canada or Mexico requiring processing at the borders, citing public health concerns.[15] This forced asylum seekers to remain restricted to

unhygienic and overcrowded refugee camps, thus making them susceptible to contracting the Covid-19 virus.

One can thus paint a (bleak) picture of the global political attitude towards refugees and asylum seekers that was adopted in light of the novel public health emergency.

Violation of the non-refoulement principle

Refugee status is not 'constitutive' but 'declaratory,' implying that a person is not required to undergo any formal assessment process to be termed as a refugee. The obligation of non-refoulement comes into play the moment a refugee steps into a state's territory or jurisdiction and harbours a genuine fear of returning to their homeland. As noted above, the application and interpretation of the Article 33(2) exception under the 1951 Refugee Convention must be done restrictively. It is quite evident that the wording of Article 33(2) does not permit blanket closure of borders and suspension of asylum procedures. It requires an *individual* to constitute a danger to national security (Court of Appeal, New Zealand, Attorney General v. Za-

---

13 Grierson, Jamie. "Kent refugee site locked down after scores test positive for Covid". The Guardian. January 19, 2021

14 Brigitte Rohwerder, "Covid-19 and the erosion of refugee protection rights" Covid Collective, June 17, 2021, https://www.covid-collective.net/covid-19-and-the-erosion-of-refugee-protection-rights/

15 "US: Covid-19 Policies Risk Asylum Seekers' Lives". Human Rights Watch, April 2, 2020, https://www.hrw.org/news/2020/04/02/us-covid-19-policies-risk-asylum-seekers-lives

oui, 2004). Thus, the general suspension of refugee status and suspension of processing applications constitutes a violation of the non-refoulement principle.

Covid-19 undoubtedly brought about a health emergency the likes of which the world had not dealt with before. States and international organisations adopted every possible measure to contain the spread of the virus and prioritise public health. States suspending their obligations of non-refoulement relied on the public health emergency to justify their actions.

However, existing jurisprudence, customary international law, and the literal interpretation of the provisions of the relevant conventions indicate that Covid-19 does not constitute a threat to security that would permit derogation from the non-refoulement obligation. Indeed, human rights experts underscored that a state's pursuit of legitimate health goals should respect the fundamental principle of non-refoulement.[16]

From a legal point of view, if states were to justify this behaviour using Article 9 of the Geneva Convention on the Status of Refugees — which allows states to undertake provisional measures to deal with grave and exceptional circumstances, which are essential to national security — it would be insufficient. Although the Covid-19 pandemic constituted a grave and exceptional circumstance, its potential to threaten national security is debatable and can only be judged on a contextual basis. Member states are mandated to respect refugees' fundamental human rights and ensure their access to healthcare facilities. Therefore, even if an asylum seeker were to test positive for Covid-19, states could not deny their fundamental rights and protections by terming them as a threat to national security. Of course, it may be argued that the risk of contagion constitutes a threat to public health at large and consequently, the security of the state. Yet there is no automatic causal link that substantiates the risk of contagion and the danger to national security.

In today's increasingly interconnected world, respect for customary international law and the international human rights law constitutes an integral part of a state's political and ethical responsibilities. States are entitled to undertake necessary measures in the interest of the welfare of their citizens, but a minimum standard of obligations to international human

---

16 Human mobility and human rights in the Covid-19 pandemic: Principles of protection for migrants, refugees, and other displaced persons, principle 6. https://zolberginstitute.org/wp-content/uploads/2020/04/Human-mobility-and-human-rights-in-the-COVID_final-1.pdf

rights law remains applicable in any circumstances. Blanket bans on the entry of asylum seekers on the grounds of public health are not in tandem with the fundamental rights guaranteed at borders. These blanket bans did not conduct the processing of individual applications and ultimately violated the principle of non-refoulement.

Conclusion

Covid-19 brought to light the shortcomings of the migratory processes at the borders of many states, which only became more pronounced during the health emergency. Refugee camps and application procedures should incorporate the infrastructure and accessibility to quality healthcare. This is not far-fetched: several states, in fact, modified their asylum procedure to suit the exigencies of the pandemic. In Indonesia, asylum seekers arriving by sea were subjected to appropriate quarantine protocols. Jordan allowed temporary access to necessary healthcare facilities and included them in the national Covid-19 vaccination plan, free of cost. Portugal initiated special measures to enable undocumented people to access public healthcare facilities and social security benefits, as available to the nationals of the country.

States–particularly those espousing values-driven governance–must undertake a detailed exploration of approaches that appropriately balance international and domestic obligations when it comes to non-refoulement during pandemics and crisis situations more broadly. Though the distinction is frequently blurred in political discourse, border control does not imply border closure. Border closure not only encourages irregular and undocumented migration without any health assessment but also deprives the state from a large percentage of human resources who could effectively contribute to reducing shortages in essential sectors.[17] Covid-19 was a borderless health emergency and states should not attempt to curb pandemics by borders alone. Such a crisis mandates the prioritisation of individual health, irrespective of their nationality or ethnicity, and requires human rights to be placed at the core of the international legal framework.

---

17 Lucas Guttentag, "Coronavirus Border Expulsions: CDC's Assault on Asylum Seekers and Unaccompanied Minors" Just Security, April 13, 2020, https://www.j ustsecurity.org/69640/coronavirus-border-expulsions-cdcs-assault-on-asylum-seeke rs-and-unaccompanied-minors/

That Covid-19 has in some ways created a 'new normal' stresses the need to integrate healthcare assessment and facilities into border control measures, and demands a human rights-based approach towards health and migration policies. It is very well understood that international norms do not permit the derogation from the non-refoulement principle on the grounds of a national emergency. As a result, despite the novel and unprecedented nature of the Covid-19 pandemic, states cannot employ it as a valid reason for violating their obligations towards refugees.

In working to create a more human and organized approach to refugees – as it has attempted to do through its Action Plan on Integration and Inclusion – the European Union must keep in mind the systemic inequities impacting refugees, including their treatment at borders. This is particularly important because the global framework for refugees is underpinned by solidarity and international cooperation to ensure that refugees can be protected, but that no state is disproportionately burdened with refugees. In the EU's case, where "solidarity is the lifeblood" such cooperation becomes a pronounced imperative within the process of integration.[18]

The EU should commit to utilising the funds available, namely the European Regional Development Fund, the Asylum and Migration Fund, and InvestEU, to improve the infrastructure at the borders and adequately train healthcare personnel to deal with an influx of refugees. Additionally, such refugees should be provided with sustainable and basic shelter facilities, including facilities to isolate and quarantine prior to the processing of their applications.

The rights of an individual must form the core of European legal instruments and refugee policy. Consequently, the EU should modify existing structures in accordance with evolving situations. Including new approaches and structural changes into policy making will not only help the European Union 'build back better' after the pandemic, but will help realize the inclusive, values-based approach that the EU envisions for itself.

Bibliography:

Al Jazeera. "Malaysia deports 1,086 Myanmar nationals despite Court order", February 23, 2021.

---

18 Opinion of Advocate General, Sharpston,, European Commission v. Republic of Hungary, Case C-718/17.

Akkerman, Mark. "Covid 19 and Border Politics", www.tni.org. Transnational Institute. November, 2020.

Brigitte Rohwerder, "Covid-19 and the erosion of refugee protection rights" Covid Collective, June 17, 2021.

Fishbein, Emily. "Fear and uncertainty for refugees in Malaysia as xenophobia escalates," The New Humanitarian. May 25, 2020, Migration.

Grierson, Jamie. "Kent refugee site locked down after scores test positive for Covid". The Guardian. January 19, 2021

Human mobility and human rights in the Covid-19 pandemic: Principles of protection for migrants, refugees, and other displaced persons, principle 6. https://zolb erginstitute.org/wp-content/uploads/2020/04/Human-mobility-and-human-right s-in-the-COVID_final-1.pdf

Human Rights Watch. "US: Covid-19 Policies Risk Asylum Seekers' Lives". April 2, 2020.

Kate Ogg and Chanelle Taoi, "Covid-19 Border Closures: A violation of non-re-foulement obligations in international refugee and human rights law", ANU College of Law Legal Studies Research Paper Series.

Lang, Hardin. "Covid-19 and the Other One Percent: An Agenda for the Forcibly Displaced Six Months into the Emergency", www.refugeesinternational.org, 15 July 2020

Lucas Guttentag, "Coronavirus Border Expulsions: CDC's Assault on Asylum Seekers and Unaccompanied Minors" Just Security, April 13, 2020, https://www.justs ecurity.org/69640/coronavirus-border-expulsions-cdcs-assault-on-asylum-seekers -and-unaccompanied-minors/

Richard Plender, *Issues in International Migration Law*, (Leiden, Brill Nijhoff, 2015)

Salvo Nicolosi, "Non refoulement during a Health Emergency", EJIL: Talk! European Journal of International Law, May 14, 2020.

Souli, Sarah. "Greece's 'new tactic' of migrant expulsion from deep inside its land borders" The New Humanitarian. October 7, 2020.

Tondo, Lorenzo. "Italy declares own ports 'unsafe' to stop migrants arriving". The Guardian. April 8, 2020.

UNHCR, Beware of long-term damage to human rights and refugee rights from the coronavirus pandemic. 2020.

Vincent Chetail, "Crisis Without Borders: What Does International Law Say About Border Closure in the Context of Covid-19?" Frontiers in Political Science, December 3, 2020.

Zahirul Bashar, Non-refoulement during Covid: Excuse for the state?", Jus Corpus Law Journal, October 30, 2021

Rethinking Refugees: The evolution of EU migration policies before and after Covid-19

Viddhi Thakker

Introduction

Migration as a phenomenon of social and economic integration has been undertaken extensively within European countries for centuries. However, due to more recent global events, the European Union has observably altered its policies on migration as part of a collective effort to accommodate people facing humanitarian crises in the world.

Nevertheless, migration has also triggered restrictions on the influx of refugees and asylum seekers into EU countries, especially when managing these displaced people is deemed too burdensome for social and economic systems. Particularly, such foundational evolution in EU migration policy has occurred twice in recent history, firstly on account of the 2015 European migration crisis and secondly, as a result of the 2020 Covid-19 pandemic. While the former dealt with a significant influx of refugees due to larger political instability in West Asian countries, the latter is dealing with a restriction in mobility across borders as a result of the highly-contagious coronavirus.

Over the past two years, the pandemic has triggered waves of restrictions; but with the impact of the pandemic subsiding, there is a need to re-evaluate the approach to migration within the EU. This paper, therefore, aims to assess the evolution of migration policies within the EU, particularly in light of the Covid pandemic and restructuring of policies in the post-Covid era.

Background

The creation of a migration policy within the European Union was introduced to develop the current state of affairs while also managing and regulating the high influx of individuals around the world migrating to this conglomerate of states. In the post-war period, these policies were introduced largely to invite guest workers to help rebuild the economy.

Over the years, however, the crux of the policies shifted focus toward highly-skilled labour and asylum seekers from war-torn countries. Since the EU's primary principle of migration policy is the principle of solidarity, it has evolved to express its preference for respect for human rights in coordination with political and social forces to solve the migration issue.

The two pivotal policy changes undertaken during this period were the Action Plan to combat Smuggling of Migrants (2015–2020) as well as the Eurozone Refugee Settlement (2015)[1]. However, EU migration policies were criticized and revamped in 2017 due to the 'vicious circle' problem: many resources were expended regulating heightened immigrant flows, but the Union still strove to follow through on its commitment to principles of human rights. This problem seems to have been exacerbated further with the onset of the coronavirus pandemic, which has amplified migration related policy issues within the EU.

The Impact of Covid on migration within the EU

As the EU was recovering from the integration of millions of refugees and migrants following the 2015 migration crisis, the Covid-19 pandemic further burdened migration processes within member states. This pandemic-related impact was felt particularly in terms of border closures, travel restrictions, and the introduction of sanitary measures to curb the spread of the virus.[2]

As opposed to strengthening measures to reduce and effectively divide the burden of refugees post-2015, EU countries introduced various reforms to mitigate the effect of the pandemic for migrants. Initially, the pandemic caused restrictions on in-person immigration and increased selective admission of migrants dependent upon job-specific profiles, primarily favoring those from health, agricultural and transportation sectors.[3]

In this context, Covid-19 restrictions temporarily halted irregular migration routes from the Mediterranean. The biggest challenge for many refugees was staying safe from the virus in overcrowded camps and centers lacking social distancing protocols, and with insufficient sanitation

---

1 "EU Migration Policy," *Council of the European Union*, (2022). https://www.consiliu m.europa.eu/en/policies/eu-migration-policy/
2 European Migration Network, *"Impact of Covid-19 in the migration area in EU,"* European Commission (2021), https://www.oecd.org/migration/mig/00-eu-emn-co vid19-umbrella-inform-en.pdf.
3 European Migration Network, *"Impact of Covid-19,"* (2021).

facilities. This situation was only worsened following the closure of sea and land borders by most states, creating a challenge for integrating these refugees into EU countries.

However, rather than entirely disrupting and altering policy approaches to migration governance, Covid-19 accelerated the existing threats of irregular, unregistered migration, thus providing an urgent platform for states to discuss solutions.[4] In accordance with the European Court of Human Rights and the Council of Europe system, the EU reformed its policies to integrate migrants without many restrictions.[5] This included automatic extension of residence permits, tolerated stays, removal of obligation to leave the country, routine suspension or extension of procedural deadlines, and lastly, a system of support for unemployed semi-skilled workers.[6]

While such efforts to mitigate the predicament of refugees and migrants as a result of the pandemic were undertaken and implemented by most EU member states, these changes proved to have a skewed effect as a result of the sheer quantity of migrants entering the Union. Prior to the pandemic, the EU naval mission IRINI actively engaged in search and rescue missions for migrants across EU country borders. However, IRINI patols decreased considerably during the pandemic, resulting in many migrant ships being stranded at sea for weeks.[7]

Migration within the EU pre-Covid

Migration within the EU operated within a policy framework largely developed throughout the 1950 s. This system, however, underwent significant change between 2015 and 2016, primarily as a result of the 'European Migration Crisis' which resulted in a massive influx of refugees from various countries across the world.

The 2011 Arab Spring resulted in a series of violent eruptions in most West Asian and African countries. Within a few years of the onset of the movement, tensions only worsened in countries like Syria and

---

4 Anna Knoll, "A Renewed Migration Contract Post Covid: What next for Migration Governance in the Mediterranean?" *European Institute of the Mediterranean*, (2020) https://www.iemed.org/publication/a-renewed-migration-contract-post-covid-what-next-for-migration-governance-in-the-mediterranean/.

5 Drahoslav Stefanek, *"Migration during a Pandemic"*, *Council of Europe* (2021). https://www.coe.int/en/web/portal/covid-19-migrants-refugees-and-asylum.

6 European Migration Network, *"Impact of Covid-19,"* *(2021)*.

7 Knoll, "A Renewed Migration Contract Post Covid" (2020).

Afghanistan, thus giving rise to full-fledged civil wars. By 2015 and 2016, this instability led to large-scale displacement resulting in a major shock to the Common European Asylum System, since the influx of about two million unauthorized migrants stretched the asylum system within the EU to its breaking point.[8]

Such a sudden, dramatic growth of refugees in the EU resulted in a faltering of its mechanisms, since border controls were unable to process the flow of migrants, resulting in an extremely skewed distribution of asylum seekers across EU countries. As a result, this European migration crisis resulted in one of the most significant revitalizations of EU migration policies to be undertaken until the Covid-19 pandemic. In light of this crisis, policy reform resulted in three major changes: first, it caused increased harmonization of rules and procedures across EU member states; second, it gave rise to a greater commitment to resettling refugees from origin regions; and lastly, it drove the establishment of a new agency to strengthen control of the EU's external borders[9].

According to Frontex, the EU's border agency, the number of unauthorized crossings into various EU countries skyrocketed from about 10,000 per year to 1.82 million in 2015[10]. The initial responses to such a dramatic growth in refugees were border closures, as Italy and Greece became the principal hotspots for migrants from West Asia and sub-Saharan Africa. Firstly, this resulted in a significant change in the policy of asylum seeking, since the 1990 Dublin Convention stipulated that the first EU country to receive the arrival of refugees would be responsible for processing asylum applications within its territory.[11] This situation was further exacerbated when Angela Merkel, then the Chancellor of Germany, propounded an 'open door policy' towards migrants, in an effort to reintegrate a virtually limitless number of refugees in her country. As a result, such a significant inflow of refugees called for urgent restructuring of migration policies within EU countries.

---

8 Tom Hatton, "European asylum policy before and after the Migration Crisis", *IZA World of Labor* (2020). https://wol.iza.org/uploads/articles/550/pdfs/european-asylum-policy-before-and-after-the-migration-crisis.pdf.

9 "EU Migration Policy," *Council of the European Union*, (2022).

10 Hatton, "European Asylum seekers" (2020).

11 Ireneusz Karolewski, Roland Benedikter, "Europe's refugee and migrant crisis," *Dans Polittique Européene* (2018), https://doi.org/10.3917/poeu.060.0098.

Reforms required for a post-Covid environment

While the pandemic caused the application of certain reforms and restrictions on migration policies across the EU, the diminishing impact of Covid-19 is now resulting in relaxations across all countries. While this may be viewed in a positive light as a continuation of the effort to integrate migrants within the EU, it is also resulting in the renewal of irregular migration and other illegal activities across European borders.

The beginning of 2020 depicted a 33 % year-on-year decrease in asylum applications and a 6-year low in irregular border crossings across EU countries.[12] However, such a drop in migration did not last for long, with irregular border crossings increasing once again within the span of a year. Similarly, smuggling networks which were disrupted in the short-term quickly regrouped, causing heightened risk to migrants traveling by sea.

In order to keep migration regulated and under control, it is imperative for EU policies to be reworked, particularly in light of changing world dynamics in the post-covid era. This could be done by further enhancing the European framework for migration and asylum management, as witnessed in the 2022 temporary protection scheme introduced by the EU for people displaced during the war in Ukraine, or through a revival of the 2015 Eurozone refugee settlement.

With a rise in migration, border controls must also be a significant priority for all member states. As a result, accelerated border procedures through Frontex are imperative; this institution can be strengthened by increasing its scope and implementation responsibilities, as well as the budget allocated towards its maintenance. Secondly, in light of the increase in irregular migration from West Asian and sub-Saharan African countries through sea routes, the European Border Surveillance System must be upgraded to provide greater scope for observation through satellite and other aerial services. In addition to monitoring irregular migration, such advanced surveillance and border control systems would also contribute greatly to curbing illegal smuggling along EU borders.[13] A combined solution for the issues of migration and other activities would involve cooperation with refugees' home countries. Such cooperation would provide a

---

12 European Commission, *"Migration statistics update: impact of Covid-19,"* (2021), https://ec.europa.eu/commission/presscorner/detail/en/IP_21_232.

13 Angeliki Dimitriadi, "The Future of European Migration and Asylum policy Post Covid-19," *Foundation for European Progressive Studies,* (2020), https://www.feps-eu rope.eu/attachments/publications/feps%20covid%20response%20migration%20as ylum.pdf.

platform for a 'global approach to migration and mobility' while strengthening cooperation with West Asian and African countries to collectively fight a system of irregular migration.[14]

The past two years, and the numerous waves of Covid-19 during this period, have gravely impacted the socio-economic wellbeing of most countries. As a result, with relaxation in restrictions and worsening conditions within home countries, EU member states are bound to witness a larger number of refugees in the upcoming years. Thus, it is imperative for the EU to implement the aforementioned changes in order to facilitate the smooth functioning of migration-related policy.

Conclusion

The migration of refugees and asylum seekers in Europe has been consistently increasing, firstly as a result of the European migrant crisis in 2015 and secondly, due to the ongoing Covid-19 pandemic. Both these situations caused a reworking of migration policies within the EU. Firstly, the 2015 crisis created a need for the revitalization of migration networks to effectively divide the burden of allocation of asylum seekers across the EU member states. However, the pandemic resulted in an alteration of restrictions. While the influx of irregular migrants reduced for a few years owing to the pandemic, it has increased gradually as the immediate impacts of the virus gradually subside. As a result, there is a need to rework migration-related policies in order to better integrate and supervise the influx of migrants within the EU. Based on the analysis of the aforementioned two phases of alteration, this paper suggests that the EU should work on accelerated border patrols, greater border surveillance especially along coastlines, and a cooperative network between migrants' host and home countries.

Bibliography

Dimitriadi, Angeliki. *The Future of European Migration and Asylum policy Post COVID-19.* Foundation for European Progressive Studies, 2020. https://www.f eps-europe.eu/attachments/publications/feps%20covid%20response%20migratio n%20asylum.pdf

---

14 Dimitriadi, "The Future of European Migration" (2020).

European Commission. *Migration statistics update: impact of COVID-19*, 2021. https://ec.europa.eu/commission/presscorner/detail/en/IP_21_232.

European Migration Network. *Impact of COVID-19 in the migration area in the EU.* European Commission, 2021. https://www.oecd.org/migration/mig/00-eu-emn-covid19-umbrella-inform-en.pdf.

Hatton, Tom. European asylum policy before and after the Migration Crisis. *IZA World of Labor*, 2020. https://wol.iza.org/uploads/articles/550/pdfs/european-asylum-policy-before-and-after-the-migration-crisis.pdf.

Karolewski, Ireneusz., and Benedikter, Roland. *Europe's refugee and migrant crisis.* Dans Polittique Européen, 2018. https://doi.org/10.3917/poeu.060.0098.

Knoll, Anna. A Renewed Migration Contract Post Covid: What next for Migration Governance in the Mediterranean? *European Institute of the Mediterranean*, 2020. https://www.iemed.org/publication/a-renewed-migration-contract-post-covid-what-next-for-migration-governance-in-the-mediterranean/.

Stefanek, Drahoslav. *Migration during a Pandemic.* Council of Europe, 2021. https://www.coe.int/en/web/portal/covid-19-migrants-refugees-and-asylum.

Towards a New Approach to European Crisis and Disaster Management

Bilal Asghar

Introduction: The EU's uneven response to Covid-19

The Covid-19 pandemic revealed a dangerous lack of disaster preparedness and crisis response capabilities across Europe. From strained healthcare systems to vulnerable supply chains, it has become evident that existing systems were unprepared for a crisis of this magnitude, and that a lack of coordination and solidarity hampered efforts.[1]

The EU's initial response was characterized as haphazard and confused, and its later efforts more akin to 'failing forward.'[2] Essential components of the disaster response, such as ensuring sufficient supply of Personal Protective Equipment (PPE) and medications, were overwhelmingly addressed independently by Member States, even though coordination would almost certainly have led to better outcomes. Some analyses have even suggested that 'sovereignty was valued over solidarity.'[3]

Although measures have since been taken to improve pandemic preparedness, a significant number of foreseeable crisis scenarios–and an unknown number of unforeseeable scenarios–could pose an even greater threat to the EU's stability. The fact that most governments have thus far relied on their militaries to act as disaster response forces should be of little comfort: Russia's brazen invasion of Ukraine helps us envision a situation in which diverting military resources to bolster civilian crisis response is simply not a viable option.[4]

Much of the post-Covid discourse has focused on preventing or mitigating future pandemics. Yet while we can certainly learn important lessons

---

1 Gray (2020) https://ec.europa.eu/research-and-innovation/en/horizon-magazine/lac k-solidarity-hampered-europes-coronavirus-response-research-finds

2 Greer et.al (2020), https://link.springer.com/chapter/10.1007/978-3-030-51791-5_44

3 Gontariuk et.al, (2021), https://www.frontiersin.org/articles/10.3389/fpubh.2021.69 8995/full

4 Pepe and Lapo (2020), IISS https://www.iiss.org/blogs/military-balance/2020/04/eur ope-armed-forces-covid-19

from the pandemic, the EU should not assume that future crises will take the same course. Indeed, such an approach runs the risk of priming EU institutions to 'fight the last war' in any future crisis, and thus hamper their response.

This essay argues that an integrated European resilience and crisis response system should be a key aspect of the EU's post-pandemic recovery efforts. Developed alongside national and local institutions, a joint initiative would help avoid redundant and duplicative systems, and would allow for more effective sharing of expertise and resources across Member States.

Significant groundwork for such a project already exists in the form of the EU's Civil Protection Mechanism and its associated organizations. But the EU must look beyond the All-Hazards Approach (AHA) currently favored by international organizations, which dangerously assumes that disasters challenge systems in similar ways. It must tailor disaster response frameworks both to risk levels and local contexts.[5] To do so, a combination of resilience initiatives is required, including both generalized and specialized initiatives that address a wide range of potential risks–natural disasters, refugee crises, hybrid threats, supply chain breakdowns, and even unforeseeable risks.

To respond effectively to future crises, the EU must equally look beyond its borders. Modern crises are increasingly globalized, and an effective framework will include key powers such as Turkey and the United Kingdom, as well as other states in the EU's neighborhood. This essay considers both EU and non-EU states within Europe, as well as the role of transatlantic and eurasian cooperation.

The essay's first section provides an outline of existing preparedness and crisis response systems across European states, as well as supranational initiatives, evaluating their recent performance to identify strengths and weaknesses. Having identified vulnerabilities, the second section draws on academic literature, technical reports, and historical examples to analyze the implications of said vulnerabilities in light of hypothetical future crisis scenarios. The essay then puts forward concrete policy proposals and recommendations, before examining potential drawbacks and objections and performing a cost-benefit analysis.

---

5   Peleg et.al (2021) https://www.sciencedirect.com/science/article/pii/S221242092100 0698?via%3Dihub#bib4

Existing preparedness and crisis response systems

Most European states maintain a variety of national disaster response institutions, based on a framework originating from the 'Civil Defence Era' centered around 'planning to reallocate the civilian population in the face of actual or potential aggression.'[6] This Civil Defence framework emphasizes doctrines, regulations, and civil-military coordination, but has been largely watered-down in Europe as the perception of such threats has decreased. To understand this framework in action, let us examine key cases of current disaster preparedness in Europe.

Germany

Germany maintains a highly developed 'civil protection' system that emphasizes coordination between Federal organizations and the Länder (states), with the Federation providing supplies and training, as well as more direct support if it is requested by local governments. This is coordinated by The Federal Ministry of the Interior, Building and Community, which supervises 2 national civil protection agencies: The Federal Office of Civil Protection and Disaster Assistance (BBK) and The Federal Agency for Technical Relief (THW). At the local level, disaster response relies on fire services, relief organizations, and over 1.8 million volunteers reinforced by professional staff, while coordination with the military is carried out at every administrative level, managed nationally by the BBK. Communication with the public is mainly centered around guidelines and publications provided by the BBK, as well as a large number of expert institutions such as the Robert Koch Institute and the GFZ German Research Centre for Geosciences.[7]

Despite the existence of these institutions, the response to Covid-19 was mainly carried out by the Federal Government and Health Ministry, advised by the Robert Koch Institute; for its part, the BBK was criticized for having failed to procure sufficient stockpiles of protective equipment. The pre-existing crisis response system was so ineffective that legislation

---

6 Kaneberg (2018) http://www.diva-portal.org/smash/get/diva2:1206379/FULLTEXT01.pdf

7 https://civil-protection-humanitarian-aid.ec.europa.eu/what/civil-protection/national-disaster-management-system/ germany_en

was passed to allow the Federal Government to override state governments to create a 'uniform' response.[8]

Spain

The Spanish approach to civil protection is based heavily on local authorities, and response coordination is escalated from local, to regional, to national authorities if the scope or severity of the crisis cannot be handled effectively at the local level. The Ministry of Interior is the highest authority in charge of Spanish civil protection, with the Directorate General of Civil Protection and Emergencies (DGPCE) coordinating and regulating the National Civil Protection System (NCPS), which attempts to integrate all public or private organizations and institutions, as well as citizens participating in civil protection. According to the European Commission's report on Spanish civil protection, 'there is no horizontal organization responsible for all prevention plans, but prevention policy is organized following a sectoral approach.'[9] In short, different types of emergencies are expected to be handled by different national, regional, and local authorities. In the context of Covid-19, this meant that pandemic response in Spain was managed through a sub-directorate of the Ministry of Health, the Centre for the Coordination of Warnings and Health Emergencies (CCAES), with support from various agencies of the Ministry of Health, the Ministry of Defence, and the national health research center, the Instituto de Salud Carlos III.[10] The national level authorities were responsible for requesting international assistance, such as activating the EU Civil Protection Mechanism.

During the early stages of the Covid-19 pandemic, this system created a degree of confusion as some local authorities attempted to impose lockdown orders which were contradicted by central government on the grounds that they did not have the authority to do so.[11] Despite the declaration of a national state of emergency, local and regional resources were not mobilized; instead, the military took on the handling of bodies,

---

8 Saurer 2020, https://www.theregreview.org/2020/05/13/saurer-covid-19-cooperativ e-administrative-federalism-germany/

9 https://civil-protection-humanitarian-aid.ec.europa.eu/what/civil-protection/natio nal-disaster-management-system/ spain_en

10 Dubin 2021, https://www.jstor.org/stable/10.3998/mpub.11927713.21?seq=1

11 https://www.elperiodico.com/es/sociedad/20200322/murcia-ordena-el-cese-de-toda -actividad-economica-no- esencial-7900635

distribution of essential resources, and tracing of case-contacts.[12] Once again, stockpiles of protective equipment were severely lacking. According to Dubin, 'the Spanish pandemic preparedness system was woefully underfunded, had few strategic reserves, and was largely unprepared to take over purchasing from the regions or even to coordinate Autonomous Communities' purchases.'[13]

Sweden

Originating from a long tradition of Civil Defence, Sweden's emergency preparedness system strongly embraces the All-Hazards Approach (AHA). The Civil Contingencies Agency (MSB) coordinates prevention, preparedness, and response across sectors and levels of government, while the responsibility for crisis and disaster management is distributed across national, regional, and local actors. Municipalities and country administrative boards have respective responsibilities within their geographical areas.[14]

Swedish crisis management doctrine is broadly guided by three principles:

- **Responsibility:** actors should retain their ordinary responsibilities in crisis situations.
- **Proximity:** crises and disasters should be managed as close as possible to those primarily concerned.
- **Similarity:** the methods and structures used in crisis and disaster management, should be as similar as possible to those used in normal circumstances.

These principles help explain why Sweden's response to Covid-19 was unusual compared to other European countries. The principle of responsibility meant that the political leadership could not override the Public Health Agency, and was instead mandated to follow their recommendations, while the principle of similarity discouraged the use of large-scale lockdowns and restrictions.[15] Despite being based on the AHA, the Swedish preparedness system did not adequately stockpile protective equipment,

---

12 https://www.telegraph.co.uk/news/2020/08/25/spain-calls-army-help-trace-covid-19 -contacts-ahead-school- reopenings/

13 Dubin (2021), https://www.jstor.org/stable/10.3998/mpub.11927713.21?seq=1

14 https://civil-protection-humanitarian-aid.ec.europa.eu/what/civil-protection/natio nal-disaster-management-system/ sweden_en

15 Pashakhanlou (2021), https://www.ncbi.nlm.nih.gov/pmc/articles/PMC8242624/

and like most countries, had to rely on the military for logistical support as well as direct medical support.[16]

EU Institutions

The EU has established a range of institutions and organizations to support Member States, associated states, as well as external states in the event of crises. This is primarily coordinated under the Union Civil Protection Mechanism (UCPM), which falls under the authority of the European Commission's Directorate-General for European Civil Protection and Humanitarian Aid Operations (DG-ECHO). The Joint Research Centre (JRC) provides Risk assessments to assist with preparedness, alongside Satellite maps produced by the Copernicus Emergency Management Service.[17] The UCPM coordinates the maintenance and use of the European Civil Protection Pool (ECPP). Since 2019, the UCPM includes the RescEU reserve force, which includes personnel and stockpiles of medical equipment. However, this is relatively small-scale: in 2021, just 11 firefighting planes and 6 helicopters were provided to the RescEU force in order to combat forest fires.[18] The UCPM has been activated a total of 540 times since 2001, and in 2021 over 60 % of the requests for assistance received were related to Covid-19, resulting in the distribution of over 200 million items of medical supplies and equipment.[19]

Overview

Examining these frameworks yields several takeaways:

- There are significant differences across countries and institutions that contribute to difficulties in communication and coordination.

---

16 https://sverigesradio.se/artikel/7435161
17 https://joint-research-centre.ec.europa.eu/scientific-activities-z/disaster-risk-manag ement_en
18 https://civil-protection-humanitarian-aid.ec.europa.eu/what/civil-protection/resce u_en
19 https://civil-protection-humanitarian-aid.ec.europa.eu/what/civil-protection/emer gency- response-coordination-centre-ercc_en

- Most disaster preparedness frameworks do not prioritize openness and do not involve the public, aside from making recommendations for individual actions and press releases.
- There is a lack of coordination and clarity with regards to decision making, chains of command, and areas of responsibility.
- Some states have excessively complex frameworks involving several layers of bureaucracy, which can hinder speed of action.
- Disaster response organizations are not generally integrated–public health being addressed by a separate ministry or institution than natural disasters, for example–and mechanisms for sharing resources across the different organizations are often inefficient or nonexistent.
- Of the countries considered, only Sweden had a clearly defined doctrine and guiding principles that it mostly adhered to them during the pandemic.

Vulnerabilities of existing frameworks and implications for future crises

The following vulnerabilities can be identified from the above analysis:

Insufficient Resources

Despite significant ongoing efforts to expand the EU's Civil Protection Pool, the overall level of resources available remains limited and not suited to addressing large-scale crises. This problem is reflected at the national level as well, with most Member States being unprepared for the pandemic and lacking the necessary stockpiles of essential equipment.

Lack of Trust in Institutions

The lack of public trust in institutions is a major challenge to any preparedness or crisis response framework as it can change the role of citizens from potential assets to threats. Given that the purpose of crisis response is to protect citizens, failing to secure trust is not only counterproductive but also contradictory to a coherent conceptual framework of resilience. In practical terms, this leads to low compliance with advised measures, a lack of cooperation with authorities, and an increased risk of demonstrations, vandalism, civil unrest, and attacks during times of crisis.

During the Covid-19 pandemic, all of these were effects observed across Europe, ranging from low compliance with mask mandates and low vaccination rates in some regions to violent protests and attacks on Covid testing and vaccination centers. The implications of this issue are wide-ranging, and given the prevalence of social media and the ease by which information contagion can occur, it is likely that mistrust will remain a key challenge during future crises.

Slow Reaction Times

Complex and unclear bureaucratic chains of command can cause significant delays in crisis response actions. This impacts some types of crises more than others; for instance, most states have a relatively clear system for the management of fires, and fire brigades are usually deployed rapidly once a fire is identified. However, complex disasters such as pandemics or supply chain breakdowns involve a large number of stakeholders, making rapid response difficult.

It is often difficult to establish whether or not a situation can actually be classified as a crisis, and waiting for the official declaration of a state of emergency can lead to the loss of valuable time. Crisis response institutions must be able to take initiative if required, however developing an adequate legal framework and sufficient checks and balances is a significant challenge.

Potential future threats

The table below provides a sample of potential future threats and the associated resources required to address them effectively. This illustrates the need for flexible and wide-ranging crisis management and preparedness.[20]

---

20 https://openknowledge.worldbank.org/handle/10986/35686

Threat	Required Resources
Extreme Heat Wave	Medical Electric Engineering
Epidemics	Medical Logistics
Critical Infrastructure Collapse	Engineering Logistics
Supply Chain Breakdown	Logistics
Industrial Accident	Engineering Firefighting Medical Logistics/Evacuation CBRN
Drought	Logistics Agricultural/Ecological
Forest Fire	Firefighting Logistics Ecological
Flood	Engineering Logistics Ecological

Concrete policy proposals and recommendations

As discussed, effectively responding to most potential threats requires flexible logistical capabilities, the availability of skills and a sufficient workforce to implement response plans, and clear communication channels with the public as well as with other stakeholders including firms, NGOs, academic institutions, and foreign governments. Below are four key recommendations on building such an effective response capability.

Recommendation 1: Clearly delineate principles and responsibilities across institutions.

Despite its controversial performance during the pandemic, Sweden's crisis management system avoided confusion caused by different authorities overriding each other and similar issues that were observed in other European nations. This can be attributed to its unique adherence to pre-defined principles and an overarching crisis response doctrine. Such principles should be established on national and transnational levels so as to both improve reaction times and increase trust in institutions.

In doing so, governments should involve all relevant stakeholders, and critically evaluate whether the All-Hazards Approach is applicable to all contexts in their crisis ecosystem. They should then establish a clear risk assessment body that would allow for the implementation of a Top-Hazards Approach (THA) in which hazards are assessed according to local risk indicators, and top-ranking hazards are prioritized in preparedness and planning activities.[21]

Recommendation 2: Increase public involvement and communication

The public should be involved with crisis preparedness and management institutions much more significantly. Currently, most public engagement is viewed through a 'crisis communication' lens, yet it is critical to change the relationship between the public and crisis management institutions from a top-down approach to a more integrated one. This can be achieved by involving the public in the preparedness phase rather than only engaging with them once a crisis has already begun. Pre-established relationships between local authorities and local businesses are also essential to a robust crisis management framework. As seen during the Covid-19 pandemic, the private sector was called upon to provide essential protective equipment, and entirely new chains of procurement had to be established on short notice. This created considerable waste, uncertainty, and mistrust, as well as opportunities for corruption. Such a situation can be avoided if local authorities are aware of the capacities of firms in their region, and establish a mutual expectation of assistance from the private sector during crises.

---

21 Bodas et.al (2020), https://www.sciencedirect.com/science/article/abs/pii/S221242 0919316358

Recommendation 3: Create national and local reserve banks of logistical capabilities, skills, and a workforce to leverage them.

This recommendation goes hand-in-hand with increasing public involvement, as opportunities to volunteer and gain skills essential to crisis management (such as basic medical knowledge) can be provided to members of the public. Furthermore, if coordinated by local authorities via community-oriented groups, these can even improve social cohesion outside of crisis situations. Individuals should be able to register the skills they have or would wish to gain, as well as personal vehicles, to be added to the local reserve bank. Incentives such as skill certificates or reductions in vehicle taxes can be provided to ensure people engage with regular exercises and are prepared to contribute in the event of a crisis.

Crises often require a wide range of skills to address effectively. For instance, a health emergency such as a pandemic requires doctors, nurses, lab technicians, and biomedical scientists, whereas responding to an earthquake requires engineers, builders, and rescue experts. Individuals possessing such skills should be involved with crisis preparedness activity and have a pre-established understanding of the system, as well as be in communication with local coordinators in order to reduce response time. Plans should also be in place for private vehicles and public transportation networks to be repurposed in order to transport essential goods to affected areas, or to evacuate residents, depending on the scale and type of disaster.

Recommendation 4: Further integrate national crisis management systems with a transnational European system.

As previously discussed, the EU's crisis management institutions are currently limited to providing small-scale, targeted assistance–and only when requested. Ongoing efforts to expand the Civil Protection Pool should continue to be supported and expanded.[22] This can be expanded to a larger scale by integrating the reserve banks of resources of neighboring countries, as well as conducting semi-regular joint exercises in a manner similar to NATO military exercises. For example, multinational teams can be sent to a region to practice rapidly establishing field hospitals.

---

22 https://erccportal.jrc.ec.europa.eu/ERCC-Response/CP-Pool#/

Objections and cost-benefit analysis

Large-scale investment in disaster preparedness can be difficult to secure due to political and economic factors. As with any investment, it has an associated opportunity cost, and political actors are often incentivised to pursue other, more visible investment opportunities. This section will address the financial cost and impact on civil liberties, outlining the objection and providing solutions that allow for preparedness to be balanced with other critical needs. It concludes with a cost-benefit analysis summarizing the points made.

Financial Cost

The literature on disaster and crisis preparedness has overwhelmingly established that the financial cost of preparedness is more than offset by the benefits in the event of a crisis. A 2016 review by Melcher established that 'the economic case for DRM across a range of hazards is strong' and that 'the benefits of investing in DRM outweigh the costs of doing so on average, by about four times the cost in terms of avoided and reduced losses.'[23] In a 2018 report for the UK government, Price found that 'economic returns associated with climate resilient development are reported in the literature as positive for the overwhelming majority of sources reviewed (i.e. BCRs in excess of 3:1 and in some cases as high as 50:1).'[24]

However, it is worth noting that these reviews include underdeveloped and disaster-prone regions, and such a dramatic return on investment may not be observed in European states. Nevertheless, given the increasing risk of climate-related disasters, as well as the backdrop of the Covid-19 pandemic–which affected all states significantly regardless of their level of economic development–it can be reasonably concluded that efforts to improve preparedness such as those suggested in this paper are overwhelmingly likely to have a positive impact.

---

23 Melcher (2016), https://link.springer.com/article/10.1007/s11069-016-2170-y
24 https://assets.publishing.service.gov.uk/media/5ab0debce5274a5e20ffe268/274_D RR_CAA_ cost_effectiveness.pdf

The Erosion of Civil Liberties: Paranoia and a Permanent State of Emergency

One drawback of such an approach that is difficult to quantify are the societal implications of a 'permanent state of emergency' that such an emphasis on crisis preparation and prevention can create. Such a state was observed following the 9/11 attacks in the United States, and very prominently during the Covid-19 pandemic, with unprecedented levels of surveillance, restrictions, and relatively unchecked executive power. These create a sense of fear and anxiety throughout the population and can have heavily detrimental effects on societal cohesion and mental health.

This is especially the case with systems based on Cold-War Era 'Civil Defence', which place an emphasis on keeping plans obfuscated from potential adversaries. Modern preparedness should not emulate these approaches. Firstly, the prevalence of social media and the advent of Open-Source Intelligence (OSINT) means that any potential adversary would likely be able to identify and exploit systems anyway. Secondly, a lack of transparency can exacerbate misinformation and create adversaries out of the general population, as shown by the prevalence of mistrust and conspiracy theories during the Covid-19 pandemic.

Of course, exceptions to this must be made in very specific crisis response plans such as those associated with terrorism or war. But there is no reason for natural disaster or pandemic preparedness not to be fully transparent. For this reason, the recommendations outlined in this essay focus on communication, the establishment of clear principles and chains of command, and the involvement of the public in resource pools. Involving the public and setting clear expectations is likely to decrease fear and anxiety while improving trust in institutions.

Cost Benefit Analysis

Costs	Benefits
Funding + Opportunity Cost	Reduction of disaster costs - Reduced unit-cost of response - Estimated benefit-to-cost ratios in the range of 3.25 – 5.31:1, and in some cases as high as 50:1.
Political Capital	Lives saved

Costs	Benefits
Potential limitation of civil liberties, e.g. through systems for requisitioning resources, vehicles.	Economic benefits of reduced uncertainty/confidence in ability to respond to crises
	Benefits to social cohesion
	Improved trust in institutions
	Reduction in crisis duration
	Creation of Jobs and Volunteer opportunities

Conclusion

The post-pandemic era provides an opportunity to learn from mistakes and significantly improve upon existing institutions and systems. Addressing the need for strong crisis management institutions and preparedness is likely to have an overall positive effect on states outside of crisis situations, and should not be seen as a waste or 'just-in case' expenditure. Instead, it should become an integral part of national and international discourse around socio-economic policymaking. Ultimately, building back better must include systems that reduce the need for 'building back' at all.

Bibliography

Badcock, James. "Spain Calls in Army to Help Trace Covid-19 Contacts Ahead of School Reopenings." *The Telegraph*, Telegraph Media Group, 25 Aug. 2020, https://www.telegraph.co.uk/news/2020/08/25/spain-calls-army-help-trace-covid -19-contacts-ahead-school-reopenings/.

Bodas, Moran, et al. "Top Hazards Approach – Rethinking the Appropriateness of the All-Hazards Approach in Disaster Risk Management." *International Journal of Disaster Risk Reduction*, vol. 47, 2020, p. 101559., https://doi.org/10.1016/j.ijdrr .2020.101559.

Dubin, Kenneth A. "SPAIN'S RESPONSE TO COVID-19." In Coronavirus Politics: The Comparative Politics and Policy of COVID-19, edited by Scott L. Greer, Elizabeth J. King, Elize Massard da Fonseca, and André Peralta-Santos, 339–60. University of Michigan Press, 2021.

Efe, El Periodico. "Murcia Rompe La Unidad y Para La Actividad No Esencial." *Elperiodico*, El Periódico, 23 Mar. 2020, https://www.elperiodico.com/es/socieda d/20200322/murcia-ordena-el-cese-de-toda-actividad-economica-no-esencial-7900 635.

European Commission. "Disaster Risk Management." *EU Science Hub*, 2021, https://joint-research-centre.ec.europa.eu/scientific-activities-z/disaster-risk-managemen t_en.

European Commission. "European Civil Protection and Humanitarian Aid Operations – Germany." *European Civil Protection and Humanitarian Aid Operations*, 2021, https://civil-protection-humanitarian-aid.ec.europa.eu/what/civil-protectio n/national-disaster-management-system/germany_en.

European Commission. "European Civil Protection and Humanitarian Aid Operations – Spain." *European Civil Protection and Humanitarian Aid Operations*, 2021, https://civil-protection-humanitarian-aid.ec.europa.eu/what/civil-protection/nati onal-disaster-management-system/spain_en.

European Commission. "European Civil Protection and Humanitarian Aid Operations – Sweden." *European Civil Protection and Humanitarian Aid Operations*, 2021, https://civil-protection-humanitarian-aid.ec.europa.eu/what/civil-protectio n/national-disaster-management-system/sweden_en.

Gontariuk, Marie, et al. "The European Union and Public Health Emergencies: Expert Opinions on the Management of the First Wave of the COVID-19 Pandemic and Suggestions for Future Emergencies." *Frontiers in Public Health*, vol. 9, 2021, https://doi.org/10.3389/fpubh.2021.698995.

Greer, S.L., de Ruijter, A., Brooks, E. (2021). The COVID-19 Pandemic: Failing Forward in Public Health. In: Riddervold, M., Trondal, J., Newsome, A. (eds) The Palgrave Handbook of EU Crises. Palgrave Studies in European Union Politics. Palgrave Macmillan, Cham. https://doi.org/10.1007/978-3-030-51791-5 _44

Gray, Richard, et al. "Lack of Solidarity Hampered Europe's Coronavirus Response, Research Finds." *Horizon Magazine*, 12 Nov. 2020, https://ec.europa.e u/research-and-innovation/en/horizon-magazine/lack-solidarity-hampered-europ es-coronavirus-response-research-finds.

Kaneberg, Elvira. "Emergency Preparedness Management and Civil Defence in Sweden: An All-Hazards Approach for Developed Countries' Supply Chains." *DIVA*, Jönköping University, Jönköping International Business School, 16 May 2018, http://www.diva-portal.org/smash/record.jsf?pid=diva2%3A1206379&dswi d=-2495.

Mechler, R. Reviewing estimates of the economic efficiency of disaster risk management: opportunities and limitations of using risk-based cost–benefit analysis. Nat Hazards 81, 2121–2147 (2016). https://doi.org/10.1007/s11069-016-2170-y

Pashakhanlou, Arash H. "Sweden's Coronavirus Strategy: The Public Health Agency and the Sites of Controversy." *National Library of Medicine*, National Center for Biotechnology Information, June 2021.

Peleg, Kobi, et al. "The COVID-19 Pandemic Challenge to the All-Hazards Approach for Disaster Planning." *International Journal of Disaster Risk Reduction*, Elsevier, 6 Feb. 2021, https://www.sciencedirect.com/science/article/pii/S221242 0921000698?via%3Dihub#bib4.

Pepe, Erica, and Amanda Lapo. "Europe's Armed Forces and the Fight against COVID-19." *IISS*, Apr. 2020, https://www.iiss.org/blogs/military-balance/2020/0 4/europe-armed-forces-covid-19.

Saurer, Johannes. "Covid-19 and Cooperative Administrative Federalism in Germany." *The Regulatory Review*, 4 June 2020, https://www.theregreview.org/2020/ 05/13/saurer-covid-19-cooperative-administrative-federalism-germany/.

UK Publishing Service. "Cost Effectiveness in Humanitarian Work Preparedness, Pre-Finnancing." *Welcome to GOV.UK*, 2021, https://www.gov.uk/.

Wirenhed, Karen. "Swedish Military Helps Combat Coronavirus – Radio Sweden." *Radio Sweden | Sveriges Radio*, Sveriges Radio, 21 Mar. 2020, https://sverigesradio. se/artikel/7435161.

Making Europe's Smart Cities Participatory: Designing for meaningful citizen engagement

Darren Wong

Introduction

The smart urbanism paradigm represents the latest incarnation of evolving urban imaginaries: a technological utopia with its roots in the 'entrepreneurial', 'informational', and 'creative' cities.[1] An infinitely malleable concept, the 'smart city' encompasses a broad range of technology-enabled urban projects across the city, such as mobility, sensors, digital services, and e-governance.[2] Harnessing technologies like artificial intelligence, the Internet of Things, data analytics, and automation, cities around the world have adopted smart urbanism as a future-oriented strategy to boost their economic competitiveness and tackle complex urban challenges.

Smart cities will continue to play a critical role in the European Union's recovery from Covid-19. Indeed, the EU has already been home to leading smart cities, with well-known examples including Zurich's Long Range Wide Area Network–which collects data to enable smart solutions to urban infrastructure challenges like air quality, water management, and parking–as well as Helsinki's mobility-as-a-service, where public transport is integrated with alternatives through the 'Whim' mobile application to streamline connectivity.[3] In fact, a recent corpus analysis found that 75 % of large EU cities proclaim to be smart cities,[4] and their spread has been

---

1 Simon Elias Bibri, Advances in the Leading Paradigms of Urbanism and their Amalgamation (Switzerland: Springer Cham, 2020)

2 The phrase 'smart city' gained traction since the mid-2000s when Cisco and IBM launched research initiatives into applying sensors, networks and analytics to urban issues.

3 Kate Pelikh, "The best smart cities in Europe", O-City, https://www.o-city.com/blo g/the-best-smart-cities-in-europe

4 Laura Alcaide Muñoz and Manuel Pedro Rodríguez Bolívar, "Tools used by citizens for participation in European smart cities", *Proceedings of the 19th Annual International Conference on Digital Government Research* (2018): https://dl.acm.org/d oi/pdf/10.1145/3209281.3225220

facilitated by multiple networks and platforms, such as the European Commission's Smart Cities Marketplace[5] and the Horizon 2020 Smart Cities and Communities programme.[6]

In November 2021, the European Commission unveiled a new mission to develop 100 climate-neutral and smart European cities by 2030 to lead urban experimentation and innovation for economic growth and climate action, paving the way for all European cities to follow suit by 2050.[7] Horizon Europe will provide initial funding of up to €1.9 billion until 2023, including €359.3 million for the Cities Mission, to facilitate implementation.

While smart cities are often shaped by the socio-political and economic agendas of techno-managerial public administrators, there has been a notable participatory turn in recent years. A growing number of initiatives are designed to empower and encourage citizens to make greater contributions as testers of new technology, policy-writers in civic hackathons, and even coders creating bottom-up solutions to urban challenges with open-source data. Terms like 'citizen-centric' and 'co-creation' have been increasingly employed, and the discursive centrality of the citizen accompanies calls from scholars for greater agency of citizens in making smart cities more meaningful and liveable. Leveraging the creativity and experiences of citizens, smart cities promise collaborative, decentralised forms of governance that promote democracy, plurality, and trust.

From a critical perspective, however, scholars have argued that the design and use of smart city technologies inevitably involve value-laden decisions about 'how societies work, and… who is expected to do what, how, where, and why.'[8] This essay seeks to unpack how digital technologies and political practices are interwoven and mobilised to advance certain agen-

5 "Towards a just and clean urban transition", Smart Cities Marketplace, accessed May 19, 2022, https://smart-cities-marketplace.ec.europa.eu/
6 "Call: Smart Cities and Communities lighthouse projects", EuroAccess, accessed May 19, 2022, https://www.euro-access.eu/calls/smart_cities_and_communities_lig hthouse_projects
7 "Commission invites cities to express their interest to become part of European Mission '100 Climate-Neutral and Smart Cities by 2030', European Commission, last modified November 25, 2021, https://ec.europa.eu/info/news/commission-invit es-cities-express-their-interest-become-part-european-mission-100-climate-neutral-an d-smart-cities-2030-2021-nov-25_en
8 Adrian Smith and Pedro Prieto-Martín, "Going Beyond the Smart City? Implementing Technopolitical Platforms for Urban Democracy in Madrid and Barcelona", *Journal of Urban Technology* (2020): 1–20

das in smart cities, focusing on citizen participation. The essay explores the role of citizens in smart cities and outlines policy pathways that anchor the EU's post-Covid push towards smart cities in sustainability and equity.

Citizen Participation in the Smart City

In response to the lack of literature dissecting the diverse ways in which citizen participation is conceptualised and enacted in the smart city, Cardullo and Kitchin developed the scaffold of smart citizen participation, modelled after Arnstein's seminal 'ladder of citizen participation.[9] Different roles of the citizen in the smart city are categorised into four forms of participation: citizen power, tokenism, consumerism, and non-participation.

Citizen power encompasses the more rewarding and representative forms of civic participation, in which citizens have greater decision-making power and ownership. Power is redistributed from traditional elites to citizens, enabling communities to negotiate and take charge of the policy and managerial aspects of smart city initiatives.

Under *tokenism*, although citizens are offered some degree of autonomy by providing feedback or suggesting alternatives, their ability to effect change is limited by the dominant framing of smart city administrators. Participation usually happens after key planning and decision-making processes have occurred.

Lower on the ladder of participation, the market rationality of the smart city is reified when citizens serve as *consumers*, selecting technological services and solutions needed for the operation of the smart city.

Finally, *non-participation* occurs when smart city administrators nudge and steer citizens towards specific behaviours, practices, and forms of conduct. Citizens are learners or data points, and initiatives require little input from citizens, who also have a low capacity to act on data. This may lead to various forms of control, including interventions, self-disciplining, and optimisation.

Apart from a few 'citizen power' initiatives rooted in the ideals of deliberative democracy, all other levels of the 'scaffold' involve post-political forms of citizen engagement. Critical scholarship has overwhelmingly

---

9 Paolo Cardullo and Rob Kitchin, "Being a "citizen" in the smart city: up and down the scaffoldof smart citizen participation", *The Programmable City Working Paper*, 30 (2017): 1–24

emphasised the civic paternalism and neoliberal logic of citizen-centric initiatives, where the roles performed by citizens advance institutional and market agendas, rather than promoting the ideals of deliberative democracy. With limited opportunities to influence decision-making, the smart city risks entrenching existing power asymmetries as participatory discourses are instrumentalised as a policy tool to promote the acceptance of smart urbanism.

The disjuncture between the discursive construction and actual dynamics of participation makes it important to interrogate the quality and outcome of citizen participation in the smart city. Being a citizen in a smart city does not necessarily make one a smart citizen. Participation is uneven and inequitable given that structural barriers, including insufficient financial resources, infrastructure, knowledge, skills, and media and technical literacy draw lines of exclusion. There is also a general lack of interest in participation due to the ambiguity of the smart city.

As digital technologies in Europe's smart cities become increasingly pervasive, city planners must also be wary of how data collection and use can create an unhealthy regime of control and efficiency. Cameras and sensors enhance the surveillance and monitoring of citizens, and the 'data'-fication of the city renders citizens into entities ready to be divided into factors for scrutiny and management.[10] The de-subjectification of citizens marks a contrast from envisioned forms of active participation; instead, citizens merely operationalise the cybernetic functions of the smart city.[11]

How then can we empower citizens to articulate their rights and create new possibilities for change in smart cities? How can policymakers develop smart cities alongside the shifting imaginaries and aspirations that citizens have for them? The following section outlines three policy approaches to better design a smart city in a way that promotes social justice, inclusion, and ownership.

---

10 Jathan Sadowski, "Selling smartness: visions and politics of the smart city", *Arizona State University*, (2016): 1–216
11 Dorien Zandbergen and Justus Uitermark, "In search of the smart citizen: republican and cybernetic citizenship in the smart city", *Urban Studies*, 57(8) (2020): 1733–1748

Policy Approach 1: Looking beyond 'co-creation'

First, policymakers should avoid linear, hierarchical thinking that romanticizes bottom-up participation. Conventionally 'empowering' forms of co-creation may bring minimal returns despite significant investments in time and energy, and often still align with technocratic governance.[12] Co-creation may be expected to complement urban governance instead of increasing ownership of citizens' data to create social or political change. Thorny issues around the ethics of data collection, surveillance, and accountability are often circumvented by eliciting feedback and inviting citizens to co-create in sanitised and politically curated spaces.

Instead, policies should recognise how local socio-political and economic circumstances create different inflections of citizen participation. The rationale, impetus, and implementation of smart cities are contingent on the diverse historical and cultural legacies, economies, governance, and political structures of places.[13] Therefore, policy learning between smart city policies and initiatives should not be reduced to formulaic models of what a successful smart city looks like, especially not jumping the gun to impose a participatory or co-creative slant on new urban projects without an assessed need or clear motivation for doing so.

To develop bottom-up participation more organically, Engelbert et al. argue that one approach could be engaging with existing citizen-led initiatives that might not fit the criteria for official funding for various reasons, such as projects specific to particular issues like poverty and refugees, and others with less scalable models.[14] This can lend greater visibility and influence to smart city initiatives that do not fully align with the institutionalised objectives set out by the government or private actors seeking economic opportunities. By recognising a broader range of smart city initiatives and the involvement of different communities, city planners can move away from the outcome-oriented pursuit of funding and prestige. Instead, they contribute to developing peripheral network practices that provide a stronger base for engagement by capturing the messier and more ambivalent roles of participation in the smart city outside prescribed categories.

---

12 Cardullo and Kitchin, "Being a "citizen" in the smart city", 16
13 Rob Kitchin, "The real-time city? Big data and smart urbanism", *GeoJournal*, 79(1) (2014): 1–14
14 Jiska Engelbert, Liesbet van Zoonen, Fadi Hirzalla, "Excluding citizens from the European smart city: the discourse practices of pursuing and granting smartness", Technological Forecasting and Social Change, 142 (2019): 347–353

One example of this approach could be political consumerism, where the consumption of technology can be unexpectedly empowering through the signalling function of consumer choices in decision-making.[15] With a more nuanced understanding of participation beyond co-creation, citizens can use choices to challenge objectionable institutional practices and align smart city initiatives with their interests. For instance, the (dis)use of mobile applications or the communication of inconveniences and discontent on feedback platforms are active and deliberate forms of non-participation that render visible problems. Appropriating the very values of efficiency and rationality argued to reduce the quality of participation in smart cities, political consumerism can be another pathway for performance-driven cities to consider citizens' (non-) responses to maximise resources and outcomes and be more accountable. Compared to voting, consultation, and partnerships as the typical model of political participation, this also presents additional benefits of frequency and immediacy. Challenging the framing of consumers and choices as antithetical to citizenship and rights, it is important to explore how the most meaningful modes of participation in the city are often acts and behaviours that are most familiar and accessible to the individual.

Policy Approach 2: Designing smart city initiatives for trust

As traditional 'heavy' and 'solid' hardware makes way for 'light' and 'liquid' software in smart cities, new invisible digital layers are laid over the urban landscape. Policymakers should demystify the technological sublime of smart cities and focus on building trust and communication channels with citizens, which can make or break any initiative. This is especially so because many aspects of smart cities like urban sensors and open data are less visible and therefore less accessible, and so are co-creative roles requiring a deeper understanding of society.

Leclercq and Rijshouwer's research on designing participatory processes analyzes three smart city initiatives in Rotterdam and designs a method to evaluate if these initiatives adequately provided citizens with the tools for participation and empowered them to create their own to sustain civic en-

---

15 Dietlind Stolle and Michele Micheletti, *Political Consumerism: Global Responsibility in Action.* (New York: Cambridge University Press, 2013)

gagement.[16] From a civic last-mile logistics platform via which youth could offer delivery services between local businesses and residents, they found that empowering intermediaries in existing networks helps mediate the perspectives of various stakeholders and renders seemingly intangible topics like digitisation and data visible and debatable. Conversely, sentiments of scepticism arose in top-down projects, where traditional state-power geometries remained and caused citizens to feel a lack of openness and loss of autonomy.

Furthermore, smart city projects tend to make long-term assumptions of trickle-down or scale effects, such as the 'inevitable' transition towards decentralised governance once the initiatives gain traction. For instance, minorities, disenfranchised, and less active stakeholders would eventually be able to access digital services and be receptive to participation like technologically savvy and entrepreneurial individuals. The instrumental approach of measuring a smart city largely indicates a static state of *smartness* at a specific time, yet policymakers should recognize that it is the accumulated experience, trust, and culture of equality and respect that will fuel continued participation in smart cities.

The incorporation of even more technological tools has been lauded as the way forward for higher-level participation, but it must also foster feelings of attachment and ownership as people find a sense of place in the myriad possible forms of the smart city. Therefore, policymakers need to evaluate which tools are most effective for authentic citizen involvement in smart cities, and the impact of these tools on trust and confidence in local governance. Two largely successful case studies include Decide Madrid and Barcelona Decidim, which are multi-functional citizen participation portals in Madrid and Barcelona respectively.[17] Offering a sliding scale of direct participation in city planning, such as debates, deliberations, proposals, and budgeting, both platforms were bolstered by a tradition of participation in district-level planning to support local meetings and information gathering. They had roots in grassroots initiatives and ground-up activism, where technology was already embraced by a willing user base to coordinate large-scale participation, support offline mobilisation, crowdfund and crowdsource initiatives, and create networks between communities. Thus, the progression from street-level activism to public institutions and back

---

16 Leclercq, E.M., Rijshouwer, E.A. Enabling citizens' Right to the Smart City through the co-creation of digital platforms. *Urban Transform* **4**, 2 (2022). https://doi.org/10.1186/s42854-022-00030-y

17 Smith and Pedro Prieto-Martín, "Going Beyond the Smart City?"

to cultivating citizen activism did not start from scratch as a top-down implementation. Beyond designing functional and responsive techno-urban environments, it is therefore important to consider how to design projects and processes that citizens trust, can relate to with their own lived experiences, and can use to participate meaningfully and deliberatively.

Policy Approach 3: Bridging the gap between citizens and policymakers

Lastly, policymakers should iteratively reflect on the role of governments in smart cities and the reasons for local governments.[18] Civil servants in the local government responsible for designing and promoting the smart city usually lack a public mandate–most instances of smart city projects are not the direct product of the policies and visions of elected political parties. The technocratic development of the smart city through city-level decision-making for broader socio-political and economic agendas may therefore clash with the aspirations and interests of citizens on the ground. One approach to advocate for the smart city and bridge this schism is to create more opportunities for interaction and dialogue between civil servants and citizens. This aims to go against the conventional mentality that relegates civil servants to evaluating policies and initiatives within the larger picture of urban governance and citizens to only participate when they are enthusiastic and skilled with a valuable contribution.

Engelbert et al. found that talking and walking as simple participatory practices can easily evoke sentiments and spark important dialogue about lived experiences in the smart city.[19] Working with the councils of the four largest cities in the Netherlands to organise 'data dialogues', citizens shared stories, feelings, possibilities, and even their prospects about the smart city. One observation was that smart urban strategies are often embedded in a policy or operational context that people already harbour preconceived notions about, and the lack of engaged communication with citizens will continue to impose barriers to access and interest in the smart city, however transparent or ethical the initiatives are.

---

18 María E. Cortés-Cediel, Iván Cantador, Manuel Pedro Rodríguez Bolívar, "Analysing citizen participation and engagement in European smart cities", *Social Science Computer Review*, 39(4) (2021): 592–626
19 Jiska Engelbert, Aksel Ersoy, Ellen van Bueren, Liesbet van Zoonen, "Capitalising on the 'public turn': new possibilities for citizens and civil servants in smart city-making", *Journal of Urban Technology*

On the other hand, civil servants–regardless of their professional role and interest in the city- lack a complete understanding of smart city technologies and hardly draw relationships between their decision-making and on-the-ground experiences for the ordinary person. Such conversations provide a necessary pause to reassess the smart city from a different vantage point, perhaps even a reality check on their decision-making. Rather than solely focusing on post-decision consensus-building, civil servants should equally pay attention to public values that are secured through the use or experimentation of smart urban technologies. By witnessing the manifestations of their decision-making first-hand and gaining insight from citizens through safe and conducive spaces for dialogue, civil servants can better execute the political will of the local citizenry and advocate for their interests in the smart city.

Conclusion

This paper has highlighted three key policy approaches that can inform more robust smart city initiative: recognising different meaningful forms of participation and agency beyond co-creation; embedding a system of trust in urban design; and bridging any value gaps between citizens and civil servants to better advocate for the smart city. To fully understand the dialectics of citizen participation in smart cities, in-depth longitudinal studies should be conducted to appreciate the dynamic fluidity of participation. Citizen roles, as framed by the state or constructed by the community and self, may be accepted, refined, supported, resented, and resisted, while shifting socio-political and economic realities redraw lines of inclusion and exclusion in the smart city.

As Europe charts a firmer path towards smart urbanism in the coming years and decades, awareness of the complex entanglements of people, places, technologies, and discourses in the smart city is critical to understanding how policies produce particular forms of subjectivities and power relations in the smart city.[20] Policies should not succumb to overly celebratory or critical perspectives of the smart city, but ground its aspirations in the desires and goals of different stakeholders in the community, and continuously learn, reflect, and adapt to improve the trust, transparency, and overall success of the smart city.

---

20 Andrew Karvonen, "Urban techno-politics: knowing, governing and imagining the city", *Science as Culture*, 29(3) (2020): 417–424